THE KEYSTONE KROWD

MACK, MABEL, THE KOPS AND THE GIRLS
(1908–1915)

BY STUART ODERMAN

THE KEYSTONE KROWD: MACK, MABEL THE KOPS AND THE GIRLS
© 2007 STUART ODERMAN
All rights reserved.

No part of this book may be reproduced in any form or by any means, electronic, mechanical, digital, photocopying or recording, except for the inclusion in a review, without permission in writing from the the publisher.

PUBLISHED IN THE USA BY:
**BearManor Media
PO Box 71426
Albany, GA 31708
www.BearManorMedia.com**

LIBRARY OF CONGRESS CATALOGING-IN-PUBLICATION DATA:

Oderman, Stuart, 1940-
 The Keystone Krowd : Mack, Mabel, the Kops and the Girls (1908/1915) / by Stuart Oderman.
     p. cm.
 Includes bibliographical references.
 ISBN-13: 978-1-59393-130-8
 ISBN-10: 1-59393-130-1
 1. Keystone Film Company. I. Title.

PN1999.K4O34 2007
791.43'09--dc22
                                    2007046826

Printed in the United States.
**Cover Image: Roscoe and Minta at Keystone
Design and Layout by Valerie Thompson**

Table of Contents

ACKNOWLEDGMENTS 1
INTRODUCTION 3
BACKGROUND TO BIOGRAPH 6

THE PLAYERS
1. CHARLES CHAPLIN 11
2. THE ARBUCKLES: MINTA DURFEE AND ROSCOE (FATTY) 23
3. GLORIA SWANSON 33
4. CHESTER CONKLIN 44
5. MACK SWAIN 51
6. CHARLIE MURRAY 56

THE BANGVILLE POLICE
INTRODUCTION: IN DEFIANCE OF GRIFFITH 61
1. EDGAR KENNEDY 67
2. SLIM SUMMERVILLE 70
3. FORD STERLING 73
4. CHARLES AVERY 81
5. MACK RILEY 86
6. NICK COGLEY 87
7. BOBBY DUNN 90
8. FRED MACE 93
9. GEORGE JESKE 99
10. HANK MANN 101

AND THE GIRLS FROM BANGVILLE
1. DOT FARLEY 109
2. MABEL NORMAND 112

MACK AND MABEL
1. WALK EAST ON FOURTEENTH 119
2. THE HIDDEN WORLD BENEATH THE STREET 125
3. AT BIOGRAPH: FIRST DAYS, FIRST IMPRESSIONS 128
4. IN THE SHADOW OF THE SORCERER 136
5. SIMPLY MABEL 139
6. CHANCES 146
7. GOLDEN GATES 161
8. FROM DREAMS TO DECISIONS 165
9. THE ENDING AND THE BEGINNING 170
10. TRYING TO MATCH THE MENTOR 176
11. THE EVER-POPULAR MAE BUSCH 182
12. A PHONE CALL 187
13. MARKING TIME... 191

BIBLIOGRAPHY 195

*To Janet Sovey and Gene Brown
with love and much gratitude*

"No matter what bedlam and pandemonium we tried to create while filming *It's a Mad Mad Mad Mad World*, we'll never come near Mack Sennett and The Keystone Krowd."

— Stanley Kramer, director
Conversation with Minta Durfee Arbuckle (1963)

Acknowledgments

I considered myself very lucky and fortunate to have been in Los Angeles, playing for a series of silent films, many of which were directed by Mack Sennett.

After the lights came up, and most of the audience had left, a lady in the third row came over to the piano, and introduced herself.

"I'm Minta Durfee Arbuckle. Roscoe Conkling Arbuckle was my husband. I'd like to talk to you."

And over the next eight summers that began in 1968, she did. She certainly did. About Roscoe: the films and the marriage, the three trials, the acquittal, and the divorce, all of which were the subject of my first book.

For *this* book, I am including what Minta and her remaining contemporaries told me about Mack Sennett and the *Keystone Krowd*. Until she left us in 1975, I thought each summer would be the last summer.

What follows comes from those eight summers, and none of this could have been accomplished or even attempted without the help of these wonderful people: David Burns, Frank Capra, Chester Conklin, Allan Dwan, William K. Everson, James L. Frasher, Lillian Gish, George Jessel, Donald Mackenzie, Colleen Moore, Ann Pennington, Aileen Pringle, Billie Rhodes, Adela Rogers St. Johns, Anthony Slide, Jessica Stonely, Gloria Swanson, Blanche Sweet, Constance Talmadge, and Claire Windsor.

Specials thanks to Ken Gordon, who patiently answered my endless questions, and to Ivy and Ken Bauer, Carol Lodise, Paul Miller, Walt Santner. And the always gracious libraries: the staff at the Maplewood, New Jersey library, and the Library of the Performing Arts at Lincoln Center, New York City.

Librarians who went the extra distance: Pat Winship (Millburn, New Jersey), Joe Yransky (Donnell Library, New York City), Mary Wrighton (Jerome Library at Bowling Green State University in Ohio), and Charles and Linda D'Addario.

Introduction

Decades after his death, at the age of seventy-six at the Motion Picture Country Home in Woodland Hills, California, Canadian-born Mack Sennett, the father of motion picture slapstick comedy, is still remembered by film audiences and students. With an output of over 1,001 two-real comedies and a handful of features in the early part of the twentieth century, some of his images are of lasting impact: Mabel Normand tied to the railroad tracks by a mustached villain (Ford Sterling) and a country hick, only to be saved by racing star Barney Oldfield (*Barney Oldfield's Race for a Life*, 1913).

Another Sennett Keystone image: Keystone Kops car chases on the streets of Los Angeles, and over the Palisades overlooking the beach at Santa Monica. *Where* the Kops were going, and *why* nobody knows. Audiences were laughing too hard to look for reasons.

Mack loved to tell anyone who would listen that he made his show business debut as the rear end of a horse at New York's Bowery Theatre, a burlesque house in 1902. The twenty-two-year-old émigré from Richmond, Quebec had surrendered his operatic ambitions to sing at the Metropolitan Opera with Caruso and Melba.

He would take work anywhere, and with anyone. His only worry: that his mother would learn that he was not an *operatic* success, not an *acting* success, and he took his lunches at saloons that gave them to people without charge, provided they were downed with five-cent beer.

His rooming-house address often changed. Rather than return to Richmond, Quebec, defeated by fast-paced New York, he roomed in cramped quarters with fellow actors, often changing addresses.

The only seemingly steady work was in burlesque houses, a job you took when you were on the way up, or on the way down.

Headlining the bill at one of these houses was famed hootchy-kootchy dancer, Little Egypt, whose hip-shaking gyrations in abbreviated Arabian nights-type costumes were well known since her initial 1893 performances at the Chicago World's Fair.

By 1902, almost a decade of work behind her, the shock of Little Egypt no longer had the original impact, and she was little more than a publicity-garnering nuisance whose court appearances were given judicial dismissal.

That young, hopeful Mack Sennett was arrested and hauled off with the company on one of these occasions, and the humiliation was one of the reasons, if not the main reason, insiders said, for his constant lampooning of the police and the law in his later one- and two-reelers.

Broadway actor Fred Mace, who was a chorus boy with Mack in the 1902 musical, *A Chinese Honeymoon*, told Minta Durfee, the wife of comedian Roscoe "Fatty" Arbuckle, the *real* reason Mack was worried about the Little Egypt engagement:

> "Catherine Sinnott, Mack's mother, was a very possessive, domineering woman who supervised almost everything her son did.
>
> "Being a boilermaker was a good, honest way to make a living.
>
> "And since Mack was not going to sing in the *respectable* Metropolitan Opera Company, *why* would he want to stay in New York, living from hand to mouth in tenements, and associating with low people from the *stage?*"

Sennett, perhaps to his own surprise, or perhaps constantly eager to justify his dreams to his mother, whose responses were always encouraging with an admonition, *Don't let anybody step on your dreams*, would always send him a letter with the message:

> "Glad to hear you're a big success.
> Here's twenty dollars."

He was never encouraged to sing in front of people, and he was told by his father and his brothers that his voice sounded like a moose in a bog.

Perhaps the constant negativity had the opposite effect. Rather than discourage Mack, it increased his desire and urgency to go forward to prove himself, *to* himself.

In his lifetime, he would be in charge of one of the largest motion picture studios, create an original style of comedy, and amass a personal fortune some said that was as high as $15,000,000.

Yet, he was afraid of the honesty and intimacy of a devoted woman's love, and he would die virtually penniless and alone.

Background to Biograph

1913. Although it is a full year before the Great War had started, there are signals and warnings being felt around the world. Germany is increasing her large standing army and the government has already made plans to increase the taxes to pay for huge guns and suitable aircraft. The second Balkan war has already ended, and Austria-Hungary has told her allies to declare war on Serbia. Italy wants no part in the matter, while Russian will come to assist Serbia, also telling Austria to remain in place. Germany is not *quite* ready, and it is only a matter of time.

In New York, talk of any upcoming war is of little importance. War is a European matter, too far away from Eastern shores.

The Broadway theatre stages are enjoying a prosperous season. Al Jolson, on Sunday nights when most of the theatres are "dark," is performing for the "pros" at the Winter Garden Theatre in a one-man show of his own creation. Downtown, the Marx Brothers are doing their vaudeville with a company of nineteen in *Mister Green's Reception*. Mae West, with whom Jolson appeared in 1911, is part of the company in *Vera Violetta*.

That both will go to vaudeville stages is a choice both made by themselves. Doing eight performances in a *structured* piece can be very monotonous compared to the "free" style of being onstage alone. Mae's show-stopping turn is being seated on a chair, wiggling her hips in a very suggestive manner while singing "Rag, Rag, Rag."

While legitimate theatre and plays may be more prestigious, both West and Jolson are now in the company of fellow vaudevillians Fred and Adele Astaire, Harry Houdini, and Sarah Bernhardt, who will eventually go into the movies, and return to vaudeville on special occasions.

In the legitimate theatre, Mary Pickford and Lillian Gish & Ernest Truex will appear in *A Good Little Devil*, Viola Dana will be seen in *Poor Little Rich Girl*, and Douglas Fairbanks is playing the lead in *Hawthorne of the U.S.A.*

Nineteen-Thirteen also marks the year Mack Sennett, who has been commuting to New York from Los Angeles, where he was mentored at Biograph by D.W. Griffith, will make the big decision to return to the Los Angeles suburb of Edendale and pursue his dream of making comedies about policemen. That he has not received any endorsement from D.W. Griffith, his mentor, is of little importance. What Mack *does* have is the basic nucleus of a *commedia del arte* group that permanently revolutionizes motion picture-making: Charlie Chaplin, Chester Conklin, Roscoe "Fatty" Arbuckle and his wife, Minta Durfee, and Mack Swain. All were hired at the studio gate during the last three months of 1913.

The Players

1 Charlie Chaplin

1913, Kansas City

The cross-country tour of the Fred Karno Company, a traveling troupe of actors, comedians, and singers, has concluded its American tour in Missouri, which is unfortunately between two oceans. Had their final engagement been played on the East Coast (New York) or the West Coast (San Francisco or Los Angeles), there would not be any problems regarding returning by ship, although New York was more desirable.

Chaplin was no stranger to the United States. His first Karno tour (1910) included New York City for six weeks at the prestigious American Music Hall at the corner of 42nd Street and Eighth Avenue. Mack Sennett, then working in a Bowery burlesque house, claimed he saw Chaplin's performance uptown. While Charlie liked to tell people that he was aware that Sennett was in the audiences in his New York days, there is no record of both struggling young men ever meeting each other at either time in New York (1910 or 1913). It is the type of lore, however, that, said often enough, might eventually bear a resemblance to actuality, or make for good press agentry for future generations of movie historians.

Chaplin, having had a taste of the California weather and beaches, and the easy availability of girls on the beach, decided his future was out West. He also did not have to bear another cold English winter.

Unlike the performers of today's late-night television talk shows, the entertainers in the early part of the twentieth century could tour for years across the country, doing virtually the same act in hundreds of theatres prior to reaching the big cities. Material could

be timed. Reactions from different audiences would be quickly noticed regarding what worked or didn't work.

Fred Karno's *A Night in an English Music Hall*, sometimes called *A Night at a London Music Hall* or *A Night in a London Club*, was a proven success.

Wisely, Chaplin returned to Los Angeles where the memory of his initial appearance was still strong in Mabel Normand's memory. She constantly called him *that funny little Englishman*, and when she heard that Chaplin was back at the Empress Theatre, Mabel told Mack and the Arbuckles, with whom she was having dinner at Roscoe and Minta's home, that they should see him.

Minta recalled:

> "When Mabel was hot on the trail with an idea she had in mind regarding something, she was like a nagging mosquito in your ear.
>
> "Mack had mentioned that he had seen Charlie when he first came to New York. It was a very standard drunk act, but what was different was Charlie's costume.
>
> "He was a Lord coming back from a night out, something he had been doing in England on vaudeville stages.
>
> "He never, I don't think, even thought or mentioned using Charlie in films. Charlie was a *stage* act and he didn't know if he could build on what was a set piece of business.
>
> "But Mabel prevailed, as usual, and the four of us went.
>
> "By this time, Charlie's solo turn was polished by having played to many *American* audiences on the road, and he knew the

> differences between American and English humor.

> "Being a *Lord* to Americans meant nothing. The character was a *drunk* who was returning home.

> "The act was little more than a series of well-executed pratfalls. What made the act different was Chaplin falling from the stage into the orchestra pit. That was unheard of, because he broke through the fourth wall."

While Chaplin's turn was well-received, Mack still wasn't totally convinced about Charlie's mannerisms working on screen. Stage performers usually couldn't adjust to the demands of the lens.

Chaplin's motion picture debut was in *Making a Living* (1914), on the Keystone lot, in early January. Although Sennett was still unconvinced to Chaplin's on-camera potential, he was given a contract at a salary of $150 a week at the insistence of Mabel who saw Charlie as much more than a standard five-dollar-a-day player.

Still, Sennett was afraid to place Mabel as his leading lady.

To give this new discovery a sense of support, Chaplin's leading lady would be Minta Durfee, the wife of Roscoe Arbuckle, who was with Mabel and Sennett when they saw Chaplin's English Lord act at the Empress.

The director would *not* be Mack Sennett, but Henry Lehrman from New York. Lehrman, within his first year of employment, directed many of Sennett's one-reelers.

Minta recalled her first and lasting impression of Lehrman for several years.

> "*Henry*, although he liked to have his name pronounced *Henri*, as if he were from Paris, which he definitely was not, added the moniker '*Pathe*' to give some sort of pedigree, was assigned by Mr. Sennett to direct *Making a Living*, Charlie's first film.

"Initially, Mabel was going to co-star, but Mack had doubts about Mabel, because she was his big *investment*. Love *never* had anything to do with any of Mack's decisions. He was all business, and at the last minute, Mabel was dropped and I was thrown in. If the film didn't make it, everyone was safe, and Mack could have seen it as a way of disposing of Charlie, or putting him as an *ensemble* player, which he hoped Charlie would have refused, and taken that as a good opportunity to sail back to England, and hook onto a Fred Karno tour, where he was always a success.

"Lehrman was no more a Frenchman than Tarzan of the Apes. Lehrman was a Jew from Brooklyn who liked to put on a *beret*, affect a bad French accent, to give the impression he just stepped on the docks of New York. He'd walked around the lot, and tell everybody he had European credentials.

"*Making a Living* wasn't given the same attention that the later Chaplin efforts got. By then, Charlie had proven himself, and he was allowed to have more control of what was going on.

"Mabel was allowed to be in many of them, and Charlie, Mabel, Roscoe and I worked together in *The Rounders*, one of Keystone's best films.

"But at the beginning, and even throughout Mack's whole career, he could never spot talent. Don't get me wrong. Mack knew talent, but everything became a matter of economics. If the audience reaction was favorable, Mack was happy, and he could take control.

"It was a good way to keep some of his players happy, with a directorial credit, and someone's name *twice*, but *no* raise in pay. He was a tough man with a dollar, and he rarely took changes.

"The only real reason he made *Tillie's Punctured Romance* and *Mickey* was to pacify Mabel who wanted to get married. Mabel had become Charlie's leading lady in *Mabel's Strange Predicament*. For this film, Mack directed, but he still had Henry Lehrman as the *assistant* director. Lehrman, who has doubled as an actor in *Making a Living* and *Kid Auto Races at Venice*, could not help but notice Chaplin's rising star."

One only has to read parts of the critical opinions of Charlie's first three films.

From *Making a Living*:
"The clever player [Chaplin] who takes the role of the nervy and very nifty sharper in the third picture is a comedian of the first water…"
Moving Picture World
February 2, 1914

From *Kid Auto Races at Venice*:
"Chaplin is a born screen comedian; he does things we have never seen done on the screen before."
The Cinema
February 7, 1914

> From *Mabel's Strange Predicament*:
> "The Keystone Company never made a better contact than when they signed on Charles Chaplin, the Karno performer. It is not every variety artiste who possesses the ability to act for the camera. Chaplin not only shows that talent, he shows it in a degree which raises him at once to the status of a star performer. We do not often indulge in prophecy, but we do not think we are taking a great risk in prophesying that in six months Chaplin will rank as one of the most popular screen comedians in the world...
> *Exhibitor's Mail*
> February 9, 1914

Within the first few months of Chaplin's term of employment at Keystone (February – December 1914) and the completion of 35 films, it was obvious to him, after the completion of 15 films with Chester Conklin, that he had doubts regarding his suitability in this new medium, and his success.

Quietly, Charlie told Chester in 1914:

> "I'm going to get out of this business. It's too much for me. I'll never catch on. It's too fast for me. I can't tell what I'm doing, or what anybody wants me to do. At any rate I figure the cinema is little more than a fad. It's canned drama. What audiences really want to see is flesh and blood on the stage. I'm not sure any real actors should get caught posing for the flickers."

Griffith, Sennett, Chaplin: Each man regarded himself as a man *of the theatre*, and no matter how popular and successful motion pictures were with their audiences, the play, the "*live*" play, was still the thing!

The theatre: its playwrights and actors performed in front of a "live" audience in a structured piece of writing: a play, a revue sketch somebody wrote down what was to be done. It was rehearsed and performed, and if successful, went on tour to other places, to play for other audiences.

Sennett, in answer to Chaplin's problems regarding adjusting to a product that has to be completed at the rate of one reel a week to fill the movie houses with paying customers, tried to explain just what his "filmed bedlam and confusion" were about:

> "We have no scenario. We get an idea, then follow the natural sequence of events until it leads up to a chase."

Chaplin patiently listened, and then shook his head. He hated chases, which showed nothing of any personality, and only served to make the actor tired.

From conversations with Mabel and Roscoe at dinner over a few evenings, Minta knew that Sennett was regarding Chaplin as a challenge that he wanted to release from any further commitments.

Minta recalled:

> "Mr. Sennett ran *Making a Living* a few times, and virtually dismissed it. It was a first film, but what can Charlie actually do to save his job?
>
> "'Create something for him! Give him an identity!'
>
> "To Mack Sennett, an identity meant a *costume*, something your audience only had to see *one time*, and then remember.
>
> "'Watch Ford Sterling,' Mabel suggested. 'Look at what he wears. Look at what he does. He's a comic Dutchman!'

"Charlie realized in *Making a Living*, he does almost nothing physical. He just stands and *fumes*. Off whom was he reacting? Where was the necessary set-up for the laughs? What crisis did this character have to deal with? What character was out to get him? Who was his foil? The only foil Charlie had in his early films was the director, Henry Lehrman.

"If you look at *Making a Living* today, that Chaplin character wasn't one easily identifiable. He had no trademarks, nothing that would get a laugh from the audience from the first moment he was seen on the screen.

"Charlie's character was wearing a monocle; he had a droopy moustache, a long coat, and a silk hat, a *high* silk hat that would be worn by an *English* man-about-town type. That he was broke, that he had no money would mean nothing to Americans, if they saw his outfit. American audiences would laugh if his costume clashed with the way he responded and behave, and his *physical* actions were inherently funny.

"When Charlie saw the day's rushes, he was *horrified*. The camera didn't pick up what he was trying to do, and the film was released, and shown in theatres, he was quite upset, claiming that Lehrman deliberately butchered his efforts.

"'Nobody's really laughing,' he would say over and over to Mabel. 'Lehrman's out to get me!'

"Word got back to Mr. Sennett, who wanted to let him go, but Mabel asked to give Charlie one more try at it. After she and Mack and the Arbuckles *were* in that audience when they saw Charlie's act, and some of those same motions in the act *were* repeated on the screen?

"What could get a laugh in the theatre, and at the same time fail to transfer onto celluloid?"

Sennett, knowing that an auto race for children was going to take place on the Venice boardwalk, saw a real opportunity to make a split reel (one-half a reel to be shared with another one-half reel) film. The actors in the Chaplin film would not have a really structured script, and there would only be one chance, as the auto race was an actuality, while Charlie would be working impromptu. He would be a total stranger, a party-crasher who somehow always manages to be wherever the camera is shooting.

As before, neither Sennett nor the requested Mabel Normand would be in the film.

It was strictly Charlie, on his own, and he had to prove himself to a still-doubtful Sennett, but this time he was better prepared, with regard to his costume. Although what would eventually become his screen persona was not totally developed, one could see his attempts at trying to find a voice.

He reported to the location at Venice, clothed in baggy pants, a cane, and a derby hat. Nothing fit, or was designed to fit. It was a decided study in logical contrasts that the audience would immediately, at his first on-camera entrance, not realize that this developing, nameless tramp fellow would be part of the cinematic soul for the next three decades.

To perfect and continually develop the Tramp character, Chaplin, with the suggestions and help from fellow Keystone players, utilized the available ideas and costumes and props: a large pair of pants belonging to Roscoe Arbuckle's father, an ill-fitting derby that was the property of Minta Durfee's father, a trimmed-down moustache courtesy of Mack Swain, and a cane whose original use may have originated in the films of French *farceur*, Max Lindner.

Many of Sennett's one- and two-reelers seemed to be an improvisation of a theme often gathered from a newspaper of the day; an event was going to take place somewhere (a dance contest, the draining of the Silver Lake Reservoir, or an auto race at Venice), and he told his players, his camera crew, and his crew show up, to utilize the natural scenery of the outdoors—film *something*.

Chaplin, whose knowledge of moviemaking was still in the developmental stage with only one film behind him, knew that he couldn't survive the Keystone concept of the constant chase where there was no plan or thought.

Mountains, ledges, beaches, and fields: everybody ran up and down, and over. Unless cars, boats or bikes were available. Only a smash-up or pure exhaustion could stop the action. The essence of a Keystone comedy is dash, crash, smash and splash. His players ran after what they desired, and away from what they wanted to keep away from.

Charlie wanted no part of the chase-and-catch-or-miss school. Chases only made actors tired, and how many times can you shoot and sometimes have to shoot that sequence more than once.

The races at *Kid's Auto Races at Venice* would be observed by a late visitor, who enters from the side, as if he were one of the spectators in attendance. The race has just begun and is still in progress when the visitor *wants* to have his picture taken. He turns up wherever the camera is located. If you have ever seen a "live" *television* program being televised where spectators are in *full* view of the cameras as broadcasts are in progress, you cannot help but notice the audience trying to be "seen" on camera, a behaviorism that has not changed since 1914, when the auto races at Venice were being photographed and Chaplin's Tramp character were quite similar to our own need to be seen—almost a century later!

Chaplin explained his character as

> "…many-sided, a tramp, a gentleman, a poet, a dreamer, a lonely fellow, always hopeful of romance and adventure. He would have you believe he is a scientist, a musician, a duke,

a polo player. However, he is not above picking up cigarette butts, or robbing a baby of its candy. And of course, if the occasion warrants it, he would kick a lady in the rear—but only in extreme anger."

Knowing that his Tramp would always be developed, he further explained this character "...was unfamiliar to the Americans, and even unfamiliar to myself."

Chaplin's third film, *Mabel's Strange Predicament*, was notable for three significant reasons: Mabel Normand was included, Mack Sennett was directing, and the dreaded Henry Lehrman was *assisting* Mack Sennett. Indeed, there would come a time when Charlie would leave the studio.

Charlie did not like the speed with which Mack wanted Charlie to work. Lehrman and Charlie were at constant odds. Mack didn't know how to handle Charlie. Mabel and Mack constantly fought over Mack's control, and Lehrman and Mabel were constantly fighting over Lehrman's constant attention to her. Not all of it was professional, and Mack had other things on his mind: the running of the studio and his mother's running of him.

It was a case of two interlocking, three-sided triangles: Mack, Mabel, and Mama. And Mack, Lehrman, and Mabel...

With the filming of *His Prehistoric Past*, Chaplin decided to consider his future at Keystone. He wanted a salary of $1,000 a week, a figure Sennett said he himself never received.

Chaplin's response was quick and logical—the public doesn't line up to see a film when Sennett's name appears, but they do for Chaplin's.

Chaplin left Keystone, not bothering to say farewell. The train was heading for Chicago and the Essanay Company.

Ford Sterling had left Sennett for financial reasons. Charlie was doing the same.

The motion picture business was a *business*.

2 The Arbuckles: Minta Durfee, and Roscoe

1970. Los Angeles. From the North Coronado St. bungalow where Minta has lived with her parents since her 1925 Paris divorce from Roscoe, the drive to the Keystone studio at 1712 Allesandro Street in the Edendale district takes approximately twenty minutes if the oncoming traffic is minimal and the drivers keep their shouts from their windows to a minimum.

As we approach the driveway to the vacant, unguarded lot, Minta breaks her silence. With the exception of the still-standing older houses, the area has undergone relatively few changes. Much of the current residents are Mexican, and there are occasional Chinese take-out places interspersed amongst the *bodegas*, whose awnings brightly announced the names of the proprietors.

"This is what's left," she says, her face grim as she sees an empty overturned white metal garbage can. "Nothing like it once was. But then again, nothing ever is. Time passes and nobody will ever remember who we were, and what we did."

Her face is grim, and I wonder what is going through her mind. With a simple turn of the wheel and aiming in a new direction, we are back at the early beginnings, her beginnings, of the industry that was active almost sixty years ago.

Our automobile is the only one on the now vacant parking lot. Even though the traffic is just outside, you can hear the passing traffic, but the cars are no longer visible. Sixty years ago, the Keystone workday would have only started to begin.

"Don't mind me, Stuart," she says in the sudden period of silence between us. "I'm just thinking about how quickly all of those early years went by so quickly. And at the same time, I can remember the

Minta Durfee Arbuckle, 1915.

conversations and recall some of the actual sentences we said during on-the-lot conversations.

"And then it's suddenly over. Permanently over, except for the memory. And you never can forget that: the good and the bad of it."

She looks outside at the area where weeds have grown between the cracks in the concrete.

And then it comes back to her, with the speed of a comet.

> "Roscoe paid for the divorce, and my trip to Paris and he even gave me a fur coat. He bought me an expensive fur coat, and he paid for a male chaperone to protect me from reporters. He was always a gentleman.
>
> "But the marriage was over. I got tired of picking up after him, and going around the next day, and apologizing to the people we were with the previous evening that he might have possibly offended because he might have had too much to drink.
>
> "If I had to do it all over again, I would still marry the same man. Maybe I should have gone back to him. He asked me many times, but I knew in the back of my mind that if we ever had a fight, he would turn on me and bring up what happened at that party at the St. Francis."

She opens the door of my kelly-green Dodge Dart, and she takes a few steps down the incline that leads to a large abandoned building. Some of the windows along the bottom row have been knocked out, and some of the frames have rusted with neglect. She tries to push her head through the windowless frame, trying to make some sense out of the darkness before she brushes her hands together.

Then she speaks.

> "Old rooms and places, if they remain undisturbed, still maintain a certain *smell*. Walk into a back room of an old bookstore, and you'll understand what I mean.
>
> "I just was thinking of the others who were on this lot, and now are gone. Even the laughs are faded, but there were laughs. And plenty of them, which is why this place was such a fun place to work in."

She points to two long one-floored buildings, one on each side of a road between them.

> "Those were the dressing rooms. One for the men, one for the ladies. Two different floors. It didn't really make any difference, because we were always in each other's dressing rooms, but to the public, and reporters…
>
> "Mabel [Normand] always had her own dressing room, but she had no star on her door, at her own request. Mack wanted to indicate something, but she never knew what. If he thought Mabel was so special, he should have done the right thing by her, and married her.
>
> "Charlie Murray, who was older than we were, used to say if Mack married Mabel, Mack's *mother* would have a special dressing room with a star on the door! *She* was always his number one!"

She gestures to the empty lot beyond the two rows of buildings.

"There were a lot of nice girls here besides Mabel, girls whose names you rarely hear mentioned: Dot Farley, Phyllis Allen, Anne Luther.

"And the boys were also good fun: Edgar Kennedy, Ford Sterling, Chester Conklin...

"Both Roscoe and I came to Keystone because of Fred Mace, a friend of Roscoe's from the early days when the two of them were doing vaudeville.

"They ran into each other, and Fred said, 'There's a big shindig on Effie Street!' Those exact words: *a big shindig*. Somebody that same day told us we should go to *Allesasndro* Street if we wanted to get hired. Hired for *what*? We were just on the road, touring in stock.

"But the next day, that's exactly what we did. We went to Allesandro Street, and a big man we later were told was the *boss* (Mack Sennett) stepped out of his office, pointed a finger at us, and *spit* whatever tobacco he still had in his mouth right in front of us, never bothering to excuse himself.

"'*Eight o'clock!*'

"And then he stepped back inside his office and loudly slammed the door. Roscoe and I looked at each other, and then Roscoe knocked on the door again. That same man opened the door, and said the same thing. 'Eight o'clock!' And he slammed the door a second time.

"We were still standing in the same place a few minutes later when that door opened a *third* time. It was that same strange man, and he had another wad of tobacco in his mouth. He squinted his eyes, and yelled this time. 'EIGHT O'CLOCK! REPORT HERE AT EIGHT O'CLOCK!'

"We guessed that was it. No real audition, although we could have told him we had done more than our share of vaudeville, and more than a few plays. Roscoe had been an illustrated slides singer between the changing of the reels at nickelodeon theatres, and I had been an *end girl* (the girl at the extreme left or right) in chorus lines in Kolb and Dill shows in San Francisco.

"At the other end was Hazel Hastings, who came from a very strict Italian family who constantly watched her, and they were always afraid that she would fall in love with a bad person. Her parents always believed theatre people were bad people who made good, easy money, and they went right through it.

"Well, Hazel didn't fall in love with an actor. She fell in love with one of the *stagehands*, who was also an *actor*, and he had a *son*! The son was still a baby, still in a crib, and Hazel married the father, Lon Chaney. That boy only knew backstage life. Both of his birth parents were in show business, but she took off when she met the parents of their son, and saw they were *mutes*! The little boy grew up, and he became an actor just like his father, Lon Chaney, and Lon married

> Hazel, the end girl.
>
> "Eventually, the little boy learned the identity of his real mother, Cleva Creighton, who had tried to poison herself, and was placed in an insane asylum. It was *years* before he forgave his father, who was afraid authorities would take him away, but he was always devoted to Hazel. He supported both his *real* mother *and* Hazel!
>
> "I don't know what happened to Cleva. Probably she was institutionalized for her whole life. It was very different in those days, and there was always a certain prejudice against actor and stage people."

Feeling adjusted to her surroundings, Minta signals for us to resume our walking. We are still the only people on the lot, with only a few buildings and dilapidated sheds to be aware of our presence. A stray cat, sensing our approaching voices, leaps from an overturned garbage can, whose sudden rolling on its side sends the animal fleeing in a state of panic. Who are we to disturb their peace?

Minta stops and points at the last door on the second floor of another row of buildings. Outside the dressing room is a set of now unsteady green steps that look unsafe to climb.

Minta pauses long enough to look at, but not approach the steps. She shakes her head and remembers:

> "Boy, oh boy. If those steps could talk, what would they say!
>
> "Roscoe and I were at Keystone around the same time as Gloria Swanson and her then-husband, Wallace Beery. We used to call them, since they were always arguing on those steps outside their dressing room, in

full view of everybody, *The Battling Beerys.*

"Wally had the stage experience, but Gloria was given the larger salary. He received $30 a week, and she received $50 a week. Mack saw the possibilities for her, I guess.

"Wally was a huge boisterous man, and when they were seen together Mack thought they would have good on-camera chemistry. Roscoe and I, too, had good on-camera chemistry, but I always thought he blended better with Mabel. But the only chemistry the Beerys had was away from the camera, like *Maggie and Jiggs* of the comic strips.

"Wally was a big drinker when he *wasn't* filming, but anything could get him upset. I remember something must have happened one day they were shooting. It was an early morning fight, so it may have started, as most of theirs did, off the set, or just after they arrived. It was really loud. So loud that many of us stepped outside to watch. You would think they were arguing from a rehearsed script from a drama, it was that coordinated. But this time Wally got physical, and he pushed her away, and she tried to get her grip, and she lost her grip on the railing, and she fell down that flight of steps, and miscarried.

"That's a terrible, awful thing for any woman to experience, and unless you're a woman you can't *possibly* know what that does to you inside your head. Roscoe and I lost a baby, and we never tried for another. I was too small to carry a baby to full term. It was something I'll never forget, and I'm sure that Miss Swanson must have grieved, even though she and Wally weren't together when this occurred. We never even knew she was pregnant. They weren't even married that long.

"I think I'm safe in saying something like that. It never was publicized, because the fact of a sudden separation would be something the studios couldn't hush. If you wanted to keep your career going, and yours fans devoted, you maintained the illusion that all was happy and wonderful on Mount Olympus! Bad news was never allowed to reach the public *at the time of the actual occurrence*. Each actor that the studio had high hopes for was a *business* investment. In front of, or away from the camera.

"The studios, Mack Sennett's Keystone studio especially, were The *Fun* Factory!"

3 Gloria Swanson

"I remember Gloria Swanson from her *pudding-face* days at Keystone, and this was before I directed her [*Manhandled*] at Paramount in 1924.

"She was *never* an actress, even in her Sennett days. She conducted herself like a movie queen, which she eventually became by the time I was given the assignment. She had toughened up considerably since she had that very short marriage to her first husband [Wallace Beery], who would publicly abuse her in front of everyone. Probably it was jealousy, but he was a good actor, and had no reason to be so insecure. Unless it was out of frustration that *she* was the money-maker from the very beginning, and as a man he greatly resented that. And he knew that the lot was aware of the financial arrangement.

"We knew that he drank a great deal when he wasn't on the set, and a lot of these players did, but he also physically abused her. She'd report earlier, and the company knew that all was not well.

"Beery was also a big gambler, and he took a lot of her money until she finally *stood up*, if you could imagine a little thing like her confronting a big guy like Wally, and just said that she wasn't going to take it anymore, and walked out! What she learned from that short time she was married, and what she learned on that lot, put her in good for the rest of her career, and all of her life. She handled all of her business affairs *without* a ten-per-center, as she used to call agents. 'I'm the one who's doing the work. Why should I pay some freeloader who just stands around holding his hand out?'

"Whatever contracts she signed were checked by an attorney to make sure everything was legal and agreed to: the salary, the length of her workday, the size of her name when it was on the screen. She trusted *nobody*.

"To direct a Gloria Swanson, you don't *actually* direct her. I had to gently coax a performance out of her, and let her think she had done it without any coaxing, and *without* any help. She was, then and now, a very independent woman.

"I also directed Lillian Gish, who, in her own way, was also demanding. Both women spoke softly, but Lillian was the actress, while Gloria was the greater *personality*. And they both had their own audiences. Gloria sort of brushed away anyone who dared to mention her Sennett Bathing Beauty days.

> "As far as I'm concerned, when she left Sennett and went over to DeMille at Paramount, she was going from the *beach* to the *bathtub*! Whatever poor judgments she sometimes made were her poor judgments, and she would admit that.
>
> "'It's my face they're paying to see on that screen. If I look good, we all look good. If the results are terrible, will anybody else take the blame? I don't think so! People have a way of disappearing, and I have to clean the mess up, and start all over again!'"

Allan Dwan, in conversation with the author (1965)

1970. New York City. The Booth Theatre. Gloria Swanson's favorite topic is herself. It is, more than ever, utmost on her mind as she writes her autobiography, *Swanson on Swanson*. She is writing everything herself, she will tell you, as she holds up yellow pads of lined second sheets that are filled with scribblings and heavily penciled crossouts, which indicate she is frustrated with what she wants the reader to remember.

She explains:

> "This is not something I wanted actually to write, but I'm doing it in response to the many people who constantly ask me questions about my life, *not* necessarily about *Sunset Boulevard* of so many years ago [1950] that brought me back to the screen after a long absence.
>
> "I wasn't Paramount's first choice. I've got to be honest. They wanted Mary Pickford and Montgomery Clift. Mary turned it down, because she didn't want to play a has-been,

> and Monty refused to do a neurotic Mama's boy. So they approached me, and I said yes. And a new, younger generation *discovered* me.
>
> "But, looking at that decision now, so many years later, maybe that film was a *mixed* blessing."

Gloria Swanson has been playing in *Butterflies Are Free* for several months on the road prior to returning to New York. Her last New York engagement was in *Twentieth Century*, a revival, with Jose Ferrer, in 1951.

Gloria Swanson has not been lost for lack of work. In the intervening years, she has played in Chicago, and has always done summer theatre in plays of her own choosing that will, as in the days when she appeared in silents, serve as a showcase for her.

An acid-tongue silent film actress, who has been a close friend of Gloria's, told the author, "Gloria was never at a loss for husbands, men or money. What she did like was occasional attention. It was what she missed, and it drove her back to work. Stage work was *immediate* attention. She liked that."

According to Shubert Alley gossip, *Butterflies Are Free* would not have marked her return to the Broadway stage. Had Gloria had her druthers, she would have returned to the musical theatre (having appeared *singing* on screen in 1934, Jerome Kern's *Music in the Air*) in Jerry Herman's *Hello, Dolly!*

Leading man David Burns, who had created the role of Horace Vandergelder opposite Carol Channing in *Hello, Dolly!*, and then played with the next two succeeding Dollys (Ginger Rogers and Martha Raye) could understand Gloria Swanson's logic.

> "Here's this Academy Award actress looking for a vehicle to bring her back to a New York audience. And every lady who played Dolly has been a success, because Dolly is nostalgia for who these Dollys *once* were.

And it's a great illusion. It's right in the lyric: 'Look at the old girl *now*, fellas.' And the audience doesn't see the older broad she is now. They see what she *once was*! Why not *Gloria Swanson*?

"But what nobody took in account was the act that all of these Dollys were in *musicals*! And here's this great scene where Dolly comes *back where she belongs*. And she goes down those stairs, and every audience goes *nuts*!

"But it didn't happen that way with Gloria Swanson. You thought about it, but when she came down, nobody was there except a few people from the Merrick [producer] office, a few people who worked upstairs and who were *very* curious to see Gloria Swanson.

"Do you remember the ending of *Sunset Boulevard*? The way *Norma Desmond* walks down the steps. Well, when Swanson walked down those steps, whoever saw it put their hands over their mouths. What they saw *wasn't* Gloria. It *wasn't* Dolly. It was that lunatic Norma Desmond from *Sunset Boulevard*!

"They didn't dare tell Gloria it was like Norma Desmond. They said her voice couldn't be heard in such a large *musical* house, and they thanked her, and said they were sorry, and they hinted that doing eight performances a week in a musical isn't the same as a straight show, and I think she got the hint.

"She never thought of auditioning for a *musical* again! Quite honestly and professionally, when was the last time she sang? In a 1930s movie?"

Although I wrote the music for a Chaplin documentary (*The Eternal Tramp*, 1965) that Gloria Swanson narrated that was first shown at the Playboy Theatre in 1967, prior to being nationally televised by NET (later given new call letters: PBS), I still had to write a formal letter of request to speak to Miss Swanson.

Miss Swanson, because of the amount of ladies who want to speak to her, does *three* matinees (Wednesday, Saturday and Sunday) and tries to rest on those days between performances, and work on her memoir.

Miss Swanson would appreciate it if I would have a *specific* question to ask.

This is my *second* visit. Miss Swanson knows I will be visiting her, and that I will be visiting her, and that I will be playing for one of her films, a Mack Sennett short she made with first husband, Wallace Beery, *Teddy at the Throttle*.

I've seen the carefully arranged stills in the lobby—*Through the Years with Gloria Swanson*. I can identify the names of her leading men whose names are underneath the pictures: Rudolph Valentino, Thomas Meighan, Lionel Barrymore, Wallace Reid, and one of William Holden from *Sunset Boulevard*, her second film for which she was nominated for an Academy Award (1950). The first was *The Trespasser* (1929).

She had formed her own production company, and using the *operatic* training she had included "Love (Your Magic Spell Is Everywhere)," which was especially commissioned for the film, and served to show that not only could she speak, but she could also *sing*.

Miss Swanson's life has been lived in public view of everything she ever did. She never really had any privacy, and the questions her backstage visitors ask have to be answered, if she wants the book to sell, and *not* be another Hollywood story.

How many husbands did you have?

Were the movie magazines of that day similar to the supermarket scandal sheets of today?

Was one of your husbands a *real* Marquis?

It is clear, I am told by Miss Swanson's press agent, that she wants to be remembered as an actress, not a Sennett Bathing Beauty, or a party girl.

In the hallway outside her dressing room, one can eerily hear her answering the questions. She is a master of public relations, having supervised her own private business in addition to being one of the first actresses to have her own television show in the early days of broadcasting.

On Mack Sennett:

> "He was a penny-pinching, uneducated, vulgar man who constantly chewed tobacco and thought absolutely nothing about spitting it out, in any direction, and not giving a thought if you were in his way.
>
> "I started there. Charlie [Chaplin] and Mabel [Normand] started there. Mack really had no regard for anyone, but it was a job, and when you have little or no experience, you did anything that paid a salary—until you felt it was time to move on.
>
> "It was Wally [Beery] who heard of Mack before I did. He was doing knockabout comedy, physical comedy, which required somebody who can get a bigger laugh if he's physically big. A big person falling and taking pratfalls is more effective than a little person.
>
> "Before we went to Sennett's in Edendale, I was going extra work in Chicago for Essanay, while Wally was playing a Swedish *maid* in a *Sweedie* comedy series. The Chicago audiences loved the idea of a man, especially a large man, impersonating a woman.

> "Charlie [Chaplin] also impersonated a woman, and so would Roscoe Arbuckle. Charlie wasn't big like the other two men, but he had a mustache, and it was that mustache that put the concept across.
>
> "Fred Mace, who got Roscoe the job at Sennett's, told Wally that Sennett would see anybody coming through the gates. That's how easy it was. Easy to get hired and equally easy to be replaced. There were no unions, and the standard pay for actors was $5 a day."

Visually, the Beerys were an interesting man and wife. He was huge and domineering, and she was petite, a typical ingénue with a flair for comedy.

Both Wally and Gloria were hired, but *not* as a possible screen team in the manner of Francis X. Bushman and his future wife, Beverly Bayne. Wally, who had the greater experience at Essanay, was signed at $50 a week, while less-experienced Gloria was signed at $65.

Although Gloria wasn't aware at the time, the larger salary she was going to receive included the possibility of posing in a bathing suit on the beach.

All of the contract players, especially the ladies, were told to pose next to one of the rocks that would serve as the standard background for all of the Bathing Beauties.

The salary for each Bathing Beauty was $12 a week, with little chance of opportunity of making a transition to parts in the one- or two-reelers. That Gloria would receive $65 a week meant that she was something above the ordinary.

Gloria explained:

> "I think Mr. Sennett had the idea that I could be another Mabel Normand. Everyone was told they could be *another* Mabel Normand. I reminded Mr. Sennett that I

was hired as an *actress*, and that I wanted to have *parts*, not stand in a bathing suit in front of some rock and smile. He said I wasn't being cooperative, and Wally questioned why I was getting more money, and did extra money mean that Sennett had the right to take *certain liberties* with me.

"Sennett told me a *Sennett* Bathing Beauty just wasn't any run-of-the-mill girl. We were the movies' answer to the *Ziegfeld Follies* girls on Broadway! But I wasn't falling for any of it, and I would not allow myself to be some easily interchangeable *dum-dum*.

"I foolishly allowed myself to pose by the rocks with Blanche Mehaffey, a nice girl, who also had objections, but we both needed money. The attitude of the public hasn't changed. We were strictly fun and laughs. Like chorus girls. Like Go-Go dancers. It's all the same thing—assembly line formula.

"I didn't stay with Keystone very long. Less than two years. Part of it was due to being with Wally. *Teddy at the Throttle* still turns up, a two-reeler I made with Wally and Bobby Vernon, who was a nice boy. He understood what I was going through. You could *see* it. And those stupid Bathing Beauty poses continue to be sold, and sold, and sold in those film shops, and used in film books. I know I'm going to be forever stuck with that image.

"When the opportunity came to leave Keystone, I took it. I had learned what there was to learn, and Sennett wasn't going to deviate from that formula of the fast laugh and the chase. Sennett had made his name, and he wasn't going to change, and I wanted my chance, too. The marriage to Wally was clearly over, and I knew I needed a break, a complete break.

"I went to Paramount at the very first chance, and I made society comedies, and domestic dramas, and judging from the bags of mail, I think the public liked them.

"You want to really know why I think Sennett never tried anything else? I think he was doubly trapped—his formula for comedy, and also trying to please his mother, who never thought he had any future. That *Mickey* feature he made was just to please Mabel, who was also looking to make a name for herself. Between Mabel and his mother, he wasn't man enough to strike out on his forward.

"He was essentially a good director of the short film. Features were not for him, and I think he knew it. He was happy enough to be a part of the program. Shorts in those days were always part of the program, and he knew how to turn them out with continuing regularity. He learned from Griffith, who also began with the short film, but Griffith was never content to stay in one place. Sennett was.

"After I made *Sunset Boulevard*, I was sent all kinds of scripts with that same type of character as the lead. I was smart to turn those roles down, and to go back to the theatre where I've had my choice of plays for the summer crowds.

"What is any actor, in any era, but a saleable or *non*-saleable commodity? You have to create your own demand. All the time!"

She tilts her head, and smiles.
She is ready for her close-up.

4 Chester Conklin

1913. Like the Biograph gates on New York's East 14th Street, the Keystone gates on Allesandro Street in suburban Edendale are also the scene of hundreds of young hopefuls waiting for the opportunity for success in the infant industry that is slowly emerging. All one needs is a *face*, a certain face that the camera loves, a face that will register on the movie screen, and attract audiences who are willing to pay money to see it.

Operative voices and Shakespearean-trained actors need not apply, if they do not have a *face—that face*. Some on-the-line hopefuls will report back a few days later, hoping that their face may be what is needed that day.

One of the persistent hopefuls, he will tell magazine interviewers in later years, is diminutive Chester Conklin; small little Chester, with his trademark mustache.

When he is presented to Mack Sennett, he asks, "Can you be funny?"

Twenty-eight-year-old Chester, who has been performing in front of audiences since winning an elocution contest in his native Oskaloosa, Iowa at the age of twelve, prior to running away to join Al G. Bernes's traveling circus as a clown, has been more than hardened by the demands of the road.

He looks Sennett squarely in the eyes and answers, "I'll leave that up to you."

Hired for three dollars a day, Chester Conklin maintains the eternally innocent look that enabled him to create three lovable characters: the always assertive and spiteful *Walrus*, the less than intelligent little boy *Fishface*, who is always walking into difficult &

terrible situations, and *Droppington*, who believes he is the mater of all he surveys, and can do no wrong.

Despite a brief stay with Majestic Studios, not for any great raise in salary, but hopeful for an opportunity to test his ability in dramatic films, he returns to Keystone, having discovered that dramatic opportunities are rare, and that his roles are supporting ones—not as significant as the parts he had at Edendale.

Minta Durfee Arbuckle, with whom Chester appeared in *Cruel, Cruel, Love, Twenty Minutes of Love,* and *Caught in a Cabaret*, whose casts also included Charlie Chaplin, explained how frustrated Charlie was in attempting to act in front of a camera, while Chester seemed to take the challenges in stride:

> "Chester was working at Keystone before Chaplin, and he had had more varieties of experience than Charlie, who was much more driven and wanted to rise quickly to the top. Of course, Chaplin did, but Charlie was always trying to top himself, and was always trying to impress Mack who might see this as a reason to give a raise.
>
> "Everyone tried to impress Mack, who was a great audience, but he truly didn't understand Chaplin, who wanted to be in charge, while Chester, I felt, just wanted to be there, and offer support. Sennett wanted *pace*, and he wanted everything to be done quickly. This is what Keystone used to be."

1970. Chester Conklin has his own private bungalow at the Actors' Home in California's Woodland Hills, a few miles away from where Chester worked in Edendale decades ago as one of the Keystone Kops. Unlike many of his contemporaries who were unable to make a transition to "talkies" at the beginning of the sound era, Chester made the transition with ease, appearing in smaller roles over the years, prior to taking "extra" work in crowd scenes.

In 1966, he made his final appearance on film in *A Big Hand for the Little Lady*, starring Henry Fonda and a supporting cast eager to reminisce with him about "the old days" when they saw him when they were kids—Charles Bickford, Jason Robards.

Always amiable to university students who are using him as primary source material for their papers on the silent era, particularly the Mack Sennett days, he is used to speaking into their recorders. Most of their questions are the same, but if Chester is tired of answering them, he gives no indication. Some have actually seen a few of his films, when he is asked to recall specific moments. On some occasions, he is amazed at how much he can actually recall.

He is expecting a visit from Minta Durfee Arbuckle and the writer. Earlier the writer played for a showing of a Buster Keaton feature in the auditorium, and there was a surprise encore—Chester and Minta in *Love Speed and Thrills*, a Sennett two-reeler made in 1915.

As we enter, Chester asks, "In what nickelodeon did you find this guy?"

"He's my boyfriend," Minta answers.

Chester laughs, "I hope you can keep up with her. She's a very peppy lady."

He points to the framed photograph on the wall of the Kops all dressed in their uniforms of the era. "Can you find me?"

I walk over to the wall, and run my eyes from left to right, and back again.

"Mack felt we should have mustaches. Mustaches, he felt, were funny. He didn't want us to look alike."

I point to one of the Kops.

"He has good eyes," he laughs. "Probably from playing those films over and over again."

He gestures to the chair near the window. When he sees that I am seated and comfortable, he continues:

> "Minta took a lot of knocking around in that film, riding in that sidecar. Mack [Swain] was going after us on horseback, and we didn't really rehearse what was

> going to actually happen until they actually started filming."

Chester pauses, and looks in Minta's direction, as if this is a signal to continue. She picks up the cue, like a theatre pro.

> "That chase was done in one take. I think they used about all of it. We weren't conscious of any timing, of how long the sequence was taking, until we heard, cut!
>
> "Mr. Sennett would have a little conference of a few minutes with us before we started, and then we heard *cut*! Then all action would stop, and we'd see what we had actually done when they ran the *rushes* at the end of day. Mr. Sennett learned how to pace his time, by humming music as the action was filmed. D.W. Griffith, who was Mr. Sennett's teacher, hummed and filmed at the same time. Indoor shots always were done with music—a piano player, who had to be aware when the sequence began and ended. It saved film, which Mr. Sennett liked, because film stock wasn't cheap, and he was very thrifty."

On the subject of Gloria Swanson, with whom Chester worked in *A Pullman Bride* (1917), Chester, once described as "a myopic, inebriated little walrus, stumbling around in outsized pants," no longer smiles. It has faded, and his voice is deeper, with a hardened edge.

> "Gloria Swanson, when we were at Keystone, was an ambitious little cutie riding on the coattails of her husband who was very abusive. There were rumors that a few weeks after the marriage, and she was on

> the lot, that she came earlier, *not* because she was eager and ambitious, but that he was abusing her, hitting her, and she had to cover the bruises on her face.
>
> "There was also the story that after a beating, she was forced to abort. It was something that was whispered amongst the ladies. It was something that wasn't spoken about...unless somebody spoke about it *first*, if you know what I mean."

He looks at Minta, who nods her head in agreement, before he continues:

> "Gloria wasn't happy at Keystone from the moment she arrived. And she was only hired because Wally presented the two of them as a package. Mack took one look at her and saw a *second* Mabel Normand, which of course she had no intention of ever becoming. Gloria thought Mabel was rude and coarse."

Again, he looks at Minta. This time she speaks up:

> "Mabel was not coarse, and she was not vulgar. She was fun. All the time. It was Gloria who saw herself as a great tragedienne."

Chester continues:

> "She fought, openly fought, at every possible opportunity. Sennett made her sit on rocks, stand in front of rocks, and this is what she really hated to do: allow herself to be hugged by Mack Swain, who used to wear a stripped bathing suit that stretched around

his big, fat stomach. And that made him look even fatter."

Minta interrupts:

> "Mack Swain had a wonderful mustache and bulging eyes, and when Gloria would look away, he would finger one end of his mustache, the way old-fashioned villains would do in *Barney Oldfield's Race for a Life*. Naturally, we'd be in on the gag, and we'd start to laugh. Gloria would get angry, because she believed we were laughing at her. We weren't *really*, but the mustache bit was standard vaudeville. It was funny when that film originally came out [1931], and the bit was still good for a laugh a few years later.
>
> "Gloria had absolutely no sense of humor, and she couldn't wait until *A Pullman Bride* was finished before she walked out. Mack wasn't going to chase her. He didn't want to have to go through the same arguments, and he knew Gloria had higher ambitions.
>
> "But Wally said she would return. He just knew she would return. After just standing near rocks in a bathing suit, what else could she do? They had just finished *Teddy at the Throttle*, and he was using his *acting* as a good reason to tie her hands together just a little too tightly. Clarence Badger, the director, noticed what was happening and he called the *acting* to a *stop*! There were red marks on her wrists. Beery was not a nice man...
>
> "Well, you know what happened. Gloria went

> on to become one of DeMille's great money-makers at Paramount, and Wally went into character parts, thinking Gloria wouldn't return. She didn't..."

Chester looks out of his bungalow window. The lights along the walkway have been dimmed. It is nearly midnight. He stares into the encroaching darkness, waiting for the next words to come.

> "I had to leave Sennett, too. Not because Mack and I didn't get along. With rare exceptions, he got along with everybody. Even Chaplin, but he kept his distance, because he knew Chaplin worked at his own rhythm and pace, and he wouldn't and couldn't work at an even pace the way he did. Chaplin *thought*. We *did*.

> "*I* had to leave because I wanted to try to do other roles and not stay doing the same thing over and over again. What Mack failed to realize was that Keystone was a wonderful training ground, but we had developed what we could do and we also wanted to be in features, while Sennett, who discovered a good formula, wanted to keep on cranking out the same thing over and over. He was content to be the bottom part of the program, the part where our films were becoming time-killers until the feature, the main attraction, went on. *We* wanted to be the main attraction! We had far outgrown our baby clothes."

He looks at Minta, but she remains silent. She looks at the photograph on the wall, concentrating on Roscoe Arbuckle. Sennett's words must be registered in her mind: *Everyone here begins here, and eventually leaves me...*

5 Mack Swain

> "Charlie Chaplin was the most immediately recognizable *by face* and *by name* film actor all over the world.
>
> "Mack Swain was the most *visually arresting* Mack Sennett player, but I doubt if anyone could identify him by name, the way they could identify Charlie. Charlie was never a Keystone Kop in the *ensemble* way that Mack Swain was."
>
> —Frank Capra
> Conversation with the author (1971)

Like the other Keystone Kops, Mack Swain was a consciously created assemblage of costume and prop which rarely varied from film to film. Prior to signing with Sennett in 1913, he was active on the vaudeville circuit, with a never-passed opportunity to do legitimate theatre when the occasion arose.

Chester Conklin, on the occasion of a second visit to the Actors Home in Woodland Hills, California, explained, as best he could, Mack and their days at Keystone.

Minta Durfee Arbuckle, at Chester's request, was *not* present, in case some unexpected references, tangential as they may be, to Minta's ex-husband, and the scandal that wrecked their lives and marriage, would change and redirect the reason for this second marriage.

A second visit was an opportunity to listen to Chester uninterrupted. It was an opportunity to hear *his* side of those days at Keystone, and his partnership with Mack, and to hear about their successful screen unit of "Ambrose-Mack and Walrus-Chester."

It was a cooler day, and Chester sat on his chair outside his bungalow and recollected:

> "Charlie [Chaplin], Mack [Swain] and I came to Sennett's at Edendale around the same time [1913]. The three of us had put in our vaudeville time, and we had done our share of stock, except for Charlie, whose stage work was limited.
>
> "We didn't know each other, and I don't think we even heard of each other. Charlie was Mabel's prize, and he wasn't going to be part of the Kops, although he was in a few pictures. Mack simply put us together. He was a quick judge of character types and what would look good on the screen. He took chances and most of them were chances that turned out well.
>
> "A few years later, the 'putting together' of two different people did *very* well for Stan Laurel and Oliver Hardy. Both men had had separate careers on the vaudeville stage, and on film. Then the director, during one of the shoots, just put them together, not knowing how it would turn out. Of course it did… brilliantly in silents *and* sound.
>
> "Mack's costume and makeup got the laugh even before the action started. The two of us were physical opposites. I was short, he was tall. Mack's costume never varied—a

> huge mustache, very dark eyes which were highlighted with greasepaint. The skin area between his eyebrows and under his eyes was darkened deeply for emphasis.
>
> "And there was always a spit-curl. I don't know if you know what a spit-curl is. It's a very tight curl of hair that was pressed against the forehead or cheek. In Mack's case, it was the forehead.
>
> "And that sly look, the *leer*, that he always displayed at a woman behind her back…And he had a long coat with brass buttons, and he wore floppy shoes. I'm recalling things as they pop into my mind, you realize."

Chester draws a deep breath and tilts his head back into the high-backed chair before he continues. It is obvious he is recalling things in quick succession, and he is also aware that the author is trying to remember all he is hearing without taking notes.

Chester reaches down for a cold glass of water and takes a few long sips before he continues.

> "I should have mentioned to Minta when you were here with her that *Caught in a Cabaret* (1914), which featured Charlie, her and Mack, is still popular with the college kids because of the cast. I see a few college kids from Arthur Knight's film class at U.S.C. every once in a while who drive up to ask about working with Charlie. I always tell them that Charlie's character, like the characters we played, always remained constant. No matter the situation. The audience sensed what to expect the moment they walked inside that movie house.

"The Ambrose and Walrus were people for the time they lasted, neither *character* had much room in which to grow. The pacing of those Sennett films was fast and furious, and the character had to be developed in a few seconds, and if the audience liked the character, he only had to step in front of the camera and he had already established his persona.

"Mack, who really preferred stage acting, didn't want to be saddled with the same bits to do. But the audience liked his Ambrose, and they didn't want him to abandon him. It's a double-edged sword—a crowd-pleaser, and a career killer. Out of costume, Mack seemed to catch on the way he did with Ambrose, and yet he was a fine actor. He left Sennett's [1917] and the other studios still wanted him to be Ambrose, even if only in costume. He floated for a while, then went back to touring in *plays*, and it was Charlie [Chaplin] who brought him back in *The Gold Rush*, and the 'eating the shoe' sequence landed a lot of offers.

"He made a good transition to sound, but his career had two high points—Ambrose and *The Gold Rush*. Chaplin was very loyal to people, and like Mack Swain, he knew that a good actor has to be one who constantly grows."

6 Charlie Murray

> "Charlie Murray was older than us, and we looked up to him like a father to listen to our problems."
>
> —Minta Durfee Arbuckle
> Conversation with author (1969)

Forty-year-old Charlie Murray, who began his employment at Edendale, was clearly not someone who was standing at the gates fresh from the street and looking for any work he could get. In 1912, the year of his hiring, Murray had been a child performer at the Robinson Circus, the same organization that had been the employers of fellow Sennett player Ford Sterling.

One of eight children, Murray had worked as a clown and rider after he left his home in Centerville, Indiana. When an accident cut short any hope of continuing, he performed in medicine shows, and got work in repertory companies as an actor until he returned home to his parents.

A friendship with pal Ollie Mack resulted with the formation of Murray and Mack, a vaudeville team specializing in Irish humor, whose success increased with the writing of their own plays, which provided legitimate theatre work between vaudeville bookings.

When the Murray and Mack team dissolved in 1910, *not* because of any feuds but because both members had exhausted their possibilities as parts of a duo and wanted to work as singles, Charlie signed with Biograph in New York.

Biograph player Blanche Sweet, when asked if she had any memories of Charlie Murray, answered:

> "I have no memory of Charlie Murray at all. Mr. Griffith was cranking out one and two-reelers at that time like wheat cakes. The film historians are amazed when I tell them that they know more about us than we do.
>
> "A lot of actors, in later years, would claim they worked for Mr. Griffith, and I suppose many of them actually did. Charlie Murray could have been in one of the shorts. We all got our start at Biograph in shorts, but I don't remember if I was in any with him. We never had any billing in those early days. And I never followed too many careers except for Mary's [Pickford], and Lillian and Dorothy's. And that was because we were friends and we started around the same time.
>
> "We avoided those Sennett films. Mr. Griffith never said anything for or against Sennett. But I do believe that he, like Lillian, thought Sennett's attitude was catering to people of limited education and this attitude was going to cheapen the industry.
>
> "If you did extra work in a Sennett one or two-reeler, in those days, you certainly didn't talk about it. Especially not to actors, whose roots were in theatre."

—Blanche Sweet
Conversation with author, 1967

Charlie's appeal to his fellow players was also augmented by the fact that he was a devoted family man who liked to tell his neighbors that whatever earned was well worth it. How many people do you know are paid to have pie fights and act silly? Making audiences laugh is more rewarding than making people cry.

The Bangville Police

Introduction: In Defiance of Griffith

"It's the naive people who become the true artists. First, they have to be naive enough to believe in themselves. Then, a performer, especially an actor or an actress, must be naive enough to keep on trying, using his talent in spite of any kind of discouragement or double cross. He doesn't pay attention to setbacks. In his disenguousness he doesn't know a setback when it smites him…He doesn't change."

Mack Sennett, *King of Comedy*

The Bangville Police (1913), which quickly followed on the heels of the half-reeler, *Hoffmeyer's Legacy*, is considered to be Sennett's precursor to his highly successful Keystone Kops. Although no *costumed* Kop, as they came to be identified, is to be seen, the Sennett formula of fast, frantic and furious, which becomes the hallmark of all of his productions, is seen in the making. It is obvious that Mack has found his voice; his belief in himself is coming to fruition, deleting the discouragement from his mentor, D.W. Griffith, in the early days.

Fully aware of the camera's potential, Mack realizes that his future rested with Mabel Normand's. Blanche Sweet, who befriended Mabel when they were under contract at Griffith's Biograph, said that Mabel was:

"…only his product, his kind of product: a comedienne.

"In her defense, a lot of people who were in comedies wanted to do dramas. The clown has always wanted to play Hamlet for centuries. Frankly, I can't think of any who did.

"You did what you did well and hoped it got you work and that audiences kept paying to see you. It was another reason to quarrel with Mack, and put the engagement ring somewhere in a desk drawer until things cooled down…or Mama went away. All of his life it was always a constant three-way battle: movies, Mama or Mabel. The best he could ever hope for was two out of three. And Mabel would always lose, but she would continue to hang on…and hope."

The Bangville Police featured the immediate comedians at hand in a conscious effort to make what would be the first of Sennett's ensemble comedies: Edgar Kennedy, Slim Summerville, Mack Riley, Charlie Avery, Bobby Dunn, George Jeske, Fred Mace, and Nick Cogley.

Released on April 24, 1913, the one-half reeler, lasting six minutes, shared the bill with Murphy's *IOU*, which included Mack Sennett in the role of a stereotyped Irish policeman.

The Bangville Police involves an attractive young girl (Mabel, naturally) afraid that robbers are in her area, so she telephones the local police station. The robbers are no more than a cow in the barn in the process of giving birth. The rural members of the police force are in a state of confusion. The formula, like an O. Henry story, is set. How do they solve this problem? Will she realize the unseen person outside her door is her own gun-bearing father? Or will she think the mysterious person could be someone trying to harm her? It is a three-way confusion—the farmhand, the rural officers of the law, and her own father.

What Mabel doesn't realize, and the audience *does* realize, is the soon-to-be-born calf is an intended surprise gift from her father. In the ensuing bedlam, the automobile is blown up; the police have to complete their journey by walking. The doors to the house are locked and the property is virtually destroyed before the identity of the robbers is discovered!

The reaction of the audience was an encouraging "go ahead" to Mack to continue. Nothing is sacred, and the law can be a source of mockery and humor. Within the moviemaking world, the reactions of some of the community to Sennett's nihilistic attitudes were less than favorable.

Lillian Gish felt "…that Sennett will be a bad influence on children by seeing law enforcement as a subject for ridicule."

Billie Rhodes, the Nestor girl at Nestor Studios, had compassion for the actors: "Those Sennett people are just playing in mud and acting without any sort of script. The storyline is quite slight, and the action is little more an excuse to just run wild! For what purpose?"

Laughter, unlike drama, had not become a matter of serious discussion. Laughter meant relief, and the Sennett audience wanted to laugh.

For the moment, Sennett had proven a lot of people wrong.

Minta Arbuckle explained Sennett's reasoning:

> "I blame D.W. Griffith for Sennett's logic and reasoning regarding lengths of time for comedies. Comedies were regarded like acrobats on a vaudeville bill—they opened the program, or they sometimes were the first act after the intermission. In both cases, the audiences were still returning to their seats or just arriving at the starts.
>
> "If there were bad weather conditions and the theatre had acrobats, nobody would ever say, 'What did I miss?' Acrobats were usually time-killers, and they rounded out the program.

"When the motion picture began to be taken seriously with DeMille's *The Squaw Man*, and the stage actress Minnie Madern Fiske's *Tess of the D'Urbervilles* and Blanche Sweet in Griffith's *Judith of Bethulia*, Sennett realized that he couldn't make a *feature*. That, giving his training, he could only make short comedies, and they would always be a part of a program.

"He still kept his friendship with Griffith, and because of that friendship, he wasn't *any* sort of competition. He could always be assured of a ride. I don't think Mack ever got any respect from Griffith, but Griffith realized that movie-making was a business and it was better to have people *on* your side than *against* you.

"So long as Sennett was happy to be any part of any program, he was happy. Money was money and business was always business. And he could keep his mother happy, which was always his main ambition—to be a success in his mother's eyes.

"Mabel, aware of the off-and-on-again relationship with Mack, still remained with him, hoping that if the success was satisfactory, Mack would pop the question and, as we used to say, make an honest woman of her. Sometimes, when Mama was in town, he would *hide* [Mabel], or keep her away, if he wasn't getting along with either of them."

Mabel was aware of the changing trends and lengths of the newer films. On several occasions she fought with Mack threatening to but never leaving him.

Blanche Sweet explained:

> "Mabel wanted to be in films that ran as long as those made by D.W. Griffith. But Sennett wouldn't listen. He saw her brand of humor as less sophisticated than that of the society humor of Sidney Drew and his wife, Lucille McVey, who acted under the name Jane Morrow, and also doubled as a scenario writer. In using their own stories, they created *Mr. and Mrs. Sidney Drew*. Their comedies were more refined and were a counterpart to the rough-and-tumble antics of Mabel and Arbuckle, which was a roughhouse sort of humor.
>
> "Both of the Drews were legitimate theatre actors like Sothern and Marlowe, and they weren't off the burlesque or vaudeville circuit like a lot of the Sennett people."

Lillian Gish, who worked at Biograph at the same time as Mack Sennett, would distance herself from Sennett by constantly telling him that she and her sister, Dorothy, *were of the legitimate theatre.*

For screen comedy, particularly the Keystone comedy, to succeed, it was essential that the camera *not* be stationary. Comedy needed a moving *camera*, the better to draw the audience into the humor of the action and emphasize funny moments and expressions. The very essence of comedy depended on funny moments and reactions which the camera could emphasize.

Many times the inter-titles, strategically placed, added to the comic moment.

To succeed, Sennett would place his actors accordingly for the best *visual* impact upon their first encounter. *Fat* next to *thin*, *tall* next to *short*, *innocence* next to *suspicious*, etc. The audience would supply the rest. The ultimate goal was the instant guffaw, the sustained giggle which would erupt into a long laugh.

Because Sennett believed that comedies and comedians (until the arrival of Charlie Chaplin, whom Sennett never really understood) had no idea how long a film should last, he established the proper length, depending on the story, should be no longer than two reels.

Running longer could possibly tire the audience into silence, the worst reaction of all.

1 Edgar Kennedy

> "Edgar Kennedy is one of the few silent film actors who was able to create and sustain an entire career from a single, simple gesture—the slow burn. He was a one-faced, one expression guy, but what an expression!"

Frank Capra, director
Conversation with author, 1971

1913. *The Master of the Slow Burn* does not accidentally discover what will sustain his almost twenty-year film career until he is on line with the other hopefuls at the Sennett Studio on Alessandro Street in Edendale.

Three years earlier, he was going to be a carpenter and earn enough money to support his family, having first been a singer at an amusement park chorus in San Francisco.

With ambitions to eventually go to New York to prepare for a career singing grand opera, he was hired by Ferris Hartman, the Ziegfeld of San Francisco, whose touring companies of Gilbert and Sullivan operettas would include a young Roscoe and Minta Durfee Arbuckle.

Ed's large frame and constant exercising at the gym made him a natural for the world of boxing. Perhaps he could be The Great White Hope who could beat the champ, a black man named Jack Johnson, whose string of victories only cause racism and hatred, making sportswriters ask for the emergence of a *white* champion.

Kennedy rejected these proposals, choosing to honor his singing contracts where, despite his singing voice, he could only do chorus work. He knew, at that moment, there could be more money in prizefighting, enough money to move his family out of the tenement section in which they dwelt, but he was an honorable man and would be loyal to whoever hired him first.

Although Kennedy claimed he had matches, with Jack Dempsey and Jack Willard (which he lost), he had taken enough punches and had received enough black eyes to give motion pictures a shot.

But he still maintained his love of the sport, a reminder of the days when he was "Ed Kennedy."

There are many versions of how Edgar Kennedy was signed by Mack Sennett, the most plausible being that Kennedy, weighing 165 pounds and being six feet tall, was *visually* impressive standing at the gate. He wanted to play heavies, which would be in keeping with someone of his stature, but the word came down that the office wasn't impressed.

Kennedy, not taking a refusal very easily, reported back the next day with the same request—*Could you use me?*

Knowing that other actors were staying away from Sennett's, most likely because of the low starting salary, and the small increments that were granted reluctantly, Kennedy was more determined to be hired. Fred Mace, who had steered other actors to Keystone, suggested to Edgar that he report to the studio again, and to bring his boxing gloves.

When Kennedy showed up the next day, he was facing nineteen rough-looking boxing toughs, who looked more street-wise than ring-experienced.

After Kennedy had successfully maintained his skills with tough number four, he was given a stock actor's contract of twenty-five dollars a week.

The "slow burn," which he had used in a career that lasted almost twenty years, from silents through sound, had come about quite accidentally. Frustrated at not getting work, and being told there was nothing by the casting office, he raised his very large hand up in the air, and in the same continuous motion, struck his face and ran it down to his chin, shaking with silent rage.

Behind the desk, the people who saw this broke into laughter. Nobody had ever reacted in that manner. They usually murmured a courteous word of thanks, and quickly left.

At that moment, he was told to return to the studio the next day.

He repeated the same "slow burn" motion for a director, and he was immediately given a contract.

He was a Keystone Kop—with a slow burn.

2 Slim Summerville

"There are two kinds of history out here—movie studio and real estate."

—Jack Hupp
Beverly Hills realtor
Conversation with the author, 1969

Les Freres Taix, near the beginning or near the end of Sunset Boulevard, depending on which way you are driving from the Hollywood Freeway to the Silver Lake area, is a French restaurant. It offered a limited menu with only one daily special, and had a policy of not accepting credit cards, or ever extending any type of credit, which dated back to the early days of Keystone.

Minta Arbuckle, dining at the restaurant one early afternoon, explains:

> "Actors never had the reputation of holding onto their money very long. They always, ever since I could remember, were making and spending, since they were living vagabond lives, and were always on the road, en route to the next town.
>
> "The studio life offered some security in that there was some insurance of constant work, but for many, the old habits were hard to break. Being actors, they had to pretend

they were making more, in an effort to impress other actors and make them feel secure about their own worth.

"I guess it's the same in other professions, but the very art of acting is narcissistic of earning a living, because you are always in full public view, whether you are on a theatrical stage eight performances a week or a vaudeville stage for how many shows a day, or even on line at a supermarket. Somebody might recognize you, and may even approach you. And you are always *on*, because their dimes and dollars at the box-office are contributing to your salary. You have to be a little better dressed than they are. That's why you're on the stage, and they're not.

"And, of course, talent has a lot to do with it, too. The more money you make, the more ostentatious is your house. And then you hope for *privacy*!"

She points to what must have been a rooming house. It is pre-1920s. Six floors high and seven windows wide, it is painted a *Velveeta* yellow, and its windows are trimmed in *Del Monte* tomato paste red. Noticeably absent are automobiles. Very few of the parking spaces are filled, and there is no shopping area. Clearly there is no opportunity for anyone to go out at night for any milk, bread or newspapers. Everyone who is inside stays inside—the few elderly occupants seated at the windows are permanently frozen in defiance of time, watching the cars pull in or out of the restaurant.

Minta comments:

"My kid brother and I used to play a little game—*spot the occupant*. We'd look at the first two floors and wonder if the same people at the window were there the last time we were here.

"This was always an old people's place, except for the times when a few character actors roomed here. They were either extras or your people just starting out. If you did well, you moved on. Or you stayed there, never took any chances on a marriage, and lived an unproductive life of constant anxiety and insecurity.

"I remember when Slim Summerville first started out. He lived here, and he eventually left. Years later, *some* of us *still* called this place the *Slim Summerville house*, and we knew what they meant.

"Let's go inside."

3 Ford Sterling

"In the early years of vaudeville, a popular attraction was the dialect comedian, a performer whose appeal depended *not* on *what* he said, but the *way* he said it. It depended wholly on the particular accent—Dutch, German, Italian, Jewish, later Negro. Some of their audiences, depending on their particular ethnic background, would find it humorous, depending on their ability to become part of what was called 'The melting pot.'

"I worked in those early days with a Yiddish accent, Bert Lahr, a German accent. You had Willie Howard, Fanny Brice (long before she became Baby Snooks on radio), The Marx Bros. Whoever was the latest to come to America, with the exception of the Negro performer, because they were here first, often became the popular attraction. Butterbeans and Susie often wore a costume and used an exaggerated accent that we'd now call a *stereotype*, but it was acceptable in those days.

"You had to work to survive, and after a period of time, you gradually cut yourself away from those beginnings."

—George Jessel
Conversation with the author, 1970

1912. Taking the name *Keystone* from a railroad car, thus avoiding any copyright fees, Mack Sennett left for California with a nucleus of actors who would be the basis of a new company whose total output would be comedic: Ford Sterling, Mabel Normand, Fred Mace, and Henry Lehrman.

Unlike his mentor D.W. Griffith, who would often adapt short stories or classics as the basis of his films, Sennett would develop original material specifically geared for his company. Everything would be purposely geared to guarantee the laugh, even the titles.

Ford Sterling's timing had been developed since he was a member of the Robinson circus company in his birthplace, LaCrosse, Wisconsin. When the circus left, seventeen-year-old Fold left with them to travel across the country, billed as "Keno, the Boy Clown."

Arriving in New York, Sterling found stage work in the quickly assembled revues whose runs were capable of a week's employment at low wages, but the salary was enough to provide enough sustenance and his room-rent until he had to make the rounds again, and repeat the same process.

George Jessel explained:

> "An act, if it weren't very memorable, could always find work, if they changed their name. Before George Burns teamed up with Gracie Allen to become Burns and Allen, he was always working under a different name.
>
> "The act only had to hope somebody in the audience didn't recognize the jokes from before."

To hear Sennett tell the story of his first motion picture, "We heard our first motion picture before we saw it...A Shriner's parade…," Mabel took a doll and tried to pawn it off on every passing Shriner who might possibly be the father.

Following her was an anxious father, Ford Sterling.

It was a stroke of genius, fabricating a story that took advantage of an article Sennett happened to read in the newspaper. Sennett often repeated the tale to anyone who would listen. Since it was known he often improvised actions as the shooting progressed, nobody would bother to challenge it. Sterling, who was one of the Biograph actors hired at the East 14th Street studio, went along with the ruse.

When it was learned that such a film came out of Biograph and not Keystone, nobody paid it much attention. Mabel and Ford did indeed make *The Would Be Shriner*, but it had been shot the previous summer, but did it really matter to audiences? Minta Arbuckle, who *never* worked at Biograph in New York, often told Sennett's story about Mabel, Ford and the Shriners.

Sterling's humor easily found success with audiences. Both he and Sennett had worked in burlesque shows where the twitching eyebrow and the constant mugging was *de rigeur*.

Minta Arbuckle easily recalled Sterling's Chief Teheezal, a police captain who eventually became Chief of the Keystone Kops. Of filming *Our Daredevil Chief* (1913) she told the author:

> "Ford was easily, after he was hired, the leading comedian of the lot. Sennett liked to crank those one- and two-reelers out like clockwork, and Ford often made it easier by filming two and three a day. He would arrive, often while another film was shooting, and ask, 'What do you want me to do?' and Mr. Sennett would give him a piece of business, and Ford would just do it, get the laugh, and then go back to what he had been previously shooting.
>
> "Nobody ever thought of sound in those days. You'd have carpenters hammering

away and we learned not to hear it or be distracted by it."

What made Sterling so beloved by audiences, and often unpopular with the censors, was a series of Jewish stereotype comedies.

Cohen at Coney Island, which followed *Cohen Collects a Debt* and *Cohen Saves the Flag*, established the character of the "funny Jew." Perhaps under pressure from Jewish groups, the Coney Island film was also playing as *At Coney Island* and *Collecting the Rent*, not to incur protests. Rent may be more acceptable than *debts*.

The *Cohen* character was also *recorded* at the same time by the Victor Talking Machine vaudeville comedian Joe Hayman for audiences on both sides of the Atlantic. The most famous, although the series lasted until 1930, was the original *Cohen on the Telephone*.

While neither Sterling nor Sennett had any anti-Semitic charges or accusations hurled at them, Sterling's last effort, *Toplitzky and Company*, was a signal that ethnic humor was coming to a halt.

Toplitzky could best be described as a comedy of manners in the garment district, complete with references to body smells, adultery, bathhouses with Yiddish signs, and references to cheese-like smells emanating from the shoes of the employees, in addition to the large breasts of the women, always being furtively watched by male co-workers.

Sterling's leading lady was Mabel Normand, whose career showed no signs of suffering despite being in an "ethnic" company. Mabel would always, to the delight of her audiences, be Mabel.

Barney Oldfield's Race for a Life (June 1913) was a satire on the melodrama, and utilized more drama than comedy. It is probably the one silent film that is familiar to people who have never seen a silent film. Taking advantage of Oldfield's reputation as a driver on the racetrack, Sennett has Sterling as a mustached villain who has Mabel tied to a railroad track as he tries to destroy her by also holding a sledge hammer over her struggling body as the train approaches.

That it has appeal to today's audience is due more to the performances of Sterling and Normand than to the fame of Oldfield.

As 1913 drew to a close, Sterling grew less enthusiastic about working at Keystone. His request for a raise in salary was denied, and a new comedian on the lot had a threatening potential. Three comedians—Chester Conklin, Mack Swain and Roscoe Arbuckle—were good candidates for being the next leading/most popular man, but there was only one person whose presence was a huge threat: Charlie Chaplin.

Minta Durfee, who worked with Sterling on *Our Daredevil Chief* and *Dirty Work in a Laundry* (also known as *The Desperate Scoundrel*), recalled:

> "Ford Sterling was genuinely intimidated by Charlie. Charlie had more versatility, and he was on the way up.
>
> "If you wanted to last with Mr. Sennett, you didn't ask for a raise. Griffith was like that, and that's where Sennett learned that trick. Give your players a chance to direct or a little bigger billing, but try not to give them more money.
>
> "Griffith lost Mary Pickford, and Mack lost Ford Sterling, who was supposed to film *Cruel, Cruel, Love.* When *Cruel, Cruel, Love* went into production, the leading man was Charlie Chaplin, and I was the leading lady. It was our third film together."

Henry Lehrman also left Keystone, hoping to direct Sterling at his newly-formed Lehrman KO (Knockout) Comedies, but the association was short-lived due to clashes in temperament.

In 1915, Sterling returned to Keystone but left two years later (1917) to work for Fox, returning to a loyal Sennett the following year, hoping he could once again be the king of the lot.

By that time, Chaplin had terminated his employment at *two* studios (Essanay and Mutual) and had gone to First National, where his first film (*A Dog's Life*) was a three-reeler.

Sterling at Keystone knew his days were a thing of the past. Perhaps he shouldn't have asked for that raise. Perhaps he shouldn't have left and returned.

Perhaps he shouldn't have a left a second time.

Mr. Sennett called those people *traitors*.

Ford Sterling, in his final days, was no longer the Dutch comedian, but an elegant villain in formal dress.

He was too late. His season was over.

Perhaps an early reviewer on the *New York Dramatic Mirror* was prophetic when he wrote of Sterling's *Cohen Collects a Debt*:

> "As one sits through this eight or ten minutes of senseless, idiotic horseplay, he wonders what it is all about. Never once is the spectator allowed to grasp the thread of the story, if there is a thread, and all he is treated to is a continuous show of waving arms and prancing feet."

Contemporary critic-writer Anthony Slide, reviewing Sennett's output, believes he has discovered the reason for his success and the Sennett formula that made his films appealing to less sophisticated audiences:

> "They lacked any sort of logic; there was no legitimate reason for whatever happened on the screen. The pace at which comedy was put over was the most important thing, and this pace was maintained by the use of skillful editing, editing techniques that Sennett had learned from Griffith at Biography."

Perhaps what Griffith said to Lillian Gish early in her career at Biograph could be applied to Ford Sterling's work at Keystone:

> "Acting is a trick. It's successful when the audience doesn't catch you doing it!"

Lillian was a reliable escape artist. Ford Sterling wasn't. He wasn't *always* successful, and he was eventually being caught "acting" too frequently.

There were increasing arguments with Henry Lehrman on the set, and clashes with Sennett over denied requests for a salary raise. Some say the presence of Roscoe Arbuckle and Mack Swain and Chester Conklin was a threat.

By 1917 the Sterling brand of humor had all but disappeared as audiences had become more *Americanized*. Perhaps the threat of the War had turned audiences away from the European sense of humor, in favor of presentations that were more "home-grown."

Sterling did work, but as an "extra."

Eventually, he simply faded away in favor of progress.

Sterling, the former leading comedian at Keystone when Chaplin was originally hired, only co-starred with Charlie in one more film, *Tango Tangles*, prior to striking out on his own to form his own company with Universal.

At Keystone, his character was always the same: the scheming Dutchman whose villainy always betrays him. Yet other comedians unsuccessfully tried to imitate him. Sterling, like many others at Keystone, was also quite capable of blending with the other funny men and be part of an ensemble.

Charlie knew he could not ever be part of the assembly line. He was not a team player, preferring to develop what bits he would insert into his characterizations on his own. Often Charlie would notice, in the midst of shooting, Roscoe Arbuckle and Ford Sterling watching the work in progress.

While Chaplin and Sterling were professionally courteous on the set to each other, the general word, according to Minta Durfee, with whom both men worked, was that Charlie *acted*, and Ford *mugged* shamelessly.

As Chaplin's star was in the ascent, Sterling's growing insecurity began to increasingly slow. Mabel's judgment about the little Englishman was correct.

Sterling confided to Elmer Ellsworth, a mutual friend of both men:

"The guy [Chaplin] has baggy pants, flat feet, the most miserable, bedraggled-looking little bastard you ever saw; makes itchy gestures as though he's got crabs under his arms—but he's funny."

But he's funny. Sterling's attitude was also the attitude of Mack Sennett, although he was reluctant to admit it. Never really at home with Sennett's direction, it was increasingly obvious with each of Charlie's films that he was able to fit himself and his acting style to Sennett's assembly-line formula of contrast and catastrophe.

4 Charles Avery

"I started every new man as a Keystone Kop to see how he worked out...Anything on film made money."

—Mack Sennett
King of Comedy

1975. Los Angeles. The Hollywood Roosevelt Hotel. Actress-producer Dorothy Davenport's (Mrs. Wallace Reid) mother, Alice, was Chaplin's leading lady in his first Keystone comedy (*Making a Living*, 1914).

Making her debut in motion pictures, not in California, but in a one-reel Western in Bayonne, New Jersey, she was a well-experienced actress prior to going west.

Without pausing for breath, she can easily recall Mack Sennett's hiring habits, as well as the way he operated at his Edendale studio.

> "Sennett's place, compared to the 'wash-tub-and-sink' Centaur place, was a metropolis! He actually had a dressing room with a place where the costumes could actually be *hung* between *takes*! It wasn't a long piece of word with nails on the wall! He tried to make his studio look like a studio, my mother told me.

"But nobody ever understood the way he would hire people.

"Only he did, and sometimes I'm not too sure he did! He looked at his people and instantly gave on-the-spot instant judgments—face first, then height and body movements. And then he would ask if you had any stage or vaudeville experience. He would do that just to ask if you could respond to his quick directions. He wanted to turn out a reel a week to make his distributors happy. He constantly reminded us he had a *product* to sell, and a film to complete.

"On Mabel's say-so, he hired Charlie Chaplin, even though he wasn't totally impressed by him, and was even afraid to direct him, as Chaplin always, even the first day, had ideas of his own.

"When Charlie saw *Making a Living* and he heard Mack wanted to drop him, he asked Mabel, who was his champion from the time she and Mack saw him onstage, for help. This was an emergency, and he knew if he went back to England, after bragging that he was going to America, it was all over.

"So everyone went to the wardrobe room, which wasn't much of a place except tables of piles of clothes in various shapes, sizes and conditions. And there he tried to throw a few things together to create a character, a specific identity that audiences would recognize immediately.

"Everybody gave him something, but it was *Charles Avery's coat* that he spotted first. Charles Avery's coat, remember that! It was small sized, too small for Charlie, but he kept it, and he realized he couldn't button the three buttons because he couldn't pull it easily across his chest. He only buttoned the *top two* that splayed the bottom portion even wider across his stomach. You looked at it and you just laughed! And that was before he was finished!

"His Tramp character still wasn't completely formed. He wanted that coat, which looked like part of what *once* could have been something good, but had fallen upon hard times."

Avery and the rest of the cast were never told that *The Bangville Police* would eventually become the Keystone Kops, as Sennett's concept hadn't yet jelled. He was just experimenting and would continue to experiment until he found the right chemistry and combination that would produce the laughter he wanted from his audiences. His actors were *clowns*, like clowns in a circus which could easily be replaced, but *not* let go. They could easily be cast in another film, like actors in a repertory theatre.

When Sennett had learned that Charles Avery had had some experience touring with stock companies, whose directors' instructions were little more than, "Walk here, stand there, count to five before you say your lines," Sennett thought that Avery's success could be in giving his players directions while he (Mack) busied himself with other projects.

Avery possessed a quality that Sennett liked in employees—obedient and loyal, the same qualities he showed Griffith when Griffith was mentoring him. Charles Avery could easily rise through the ranks.

What Avery didn't anticipate was his first assignment: direct Sydney Chaplin, the half-brother of Charles, who had left

Keystone to work for Essanay in Chicago.

Minta Arbuckle, who had worked with Charlie, saw the difference between both Chaplins:

> "Charlie, even in those early days at Keystone, was a *thinker*. He often said he couldn't maintain the Sennett pace—constant motion without any reason or purpose, just keep the film going. When the opportunity came to leave, he left. Partly it was because of money. Partly it was control—Charlie wanted to have more *say* in what was being turned out.
>
> "Sydney, who would handle Charlie's finances, stayed on after Charlie left. Charles Avery was glad Mack was keeping him on. Sydney, who had options of his own, was easier going than his brother, but not always as easy to control. He wasn't stubborn or adamant in his beliefs, but he liked to make everyone laugh by saying off-color remarks, which made the lip-readers howl when the day's 'rushes' were later reviewed.
>
> "Perhaps Sydney wanted to establish his *own* identity now that Charlie was gone. To Avery's credit, he knew to re-cut the action and delete the remarks. Miraculously, the film always was completed, edited and shown to Mr. Sennett on the day and time it was to be exhibited. Mack knew all artists and players had varying temperaments, and he knew when to step in and when to stay away.
>
> "Sydney was never as successful as Charlie; it

didn't matter that much to Mack, even though Charlie had left. Ford Sterling had gone, and in came Charlie, and Chaplin's name was still on the billboard. Mack was never really that crazy about Charlie. A Chaplin was still a Chaplin.

"He was still holding onto Mabel without ever making any sustained commitment. Occasionally they would fight, and then part for a day or two, but she would return always hoping for a change...

"Avery was always very dependable, and he would turn out a satisfactory workmanlike product, which was all that Mack really wanted. Avery would spend time with Mack as Mack would spend time with Griffith. In saving Avery, he was developing an ally. Mack knew he needed an ally to enable Mack to be always in charge, even if only for a few moments!"

5 Mack Riley

"It wasn't me, the Old Man, who was so funny; it was the comical people I had around me. I called myself *King of Comedy.*

"I seldom needed to say much to my writers, gag men and actors...Every other talented person whoever worked for me: Ben Turpin, Roscoe Arbuckle, Harry Langdon, Buster Keaton, Charles Murray, Gloria Swanson, Charlie Chaplin, Harold Lloyd, even Mabel Normand eventually flew my roost.

"Start with Sennett, and get rich somewhere else!"

—Mack Sennett, *King of Comedy*

With the release of *The Bangville Police*, on April 24, 1913, Sennett's idea of a police force, first seen in *Hoffmeyer's Legacy*, a half-reeler released the previous December, became a viable reality.

In neither film did the actors become what have been identifiable as the *Keystone* Kops.

Both casts, with the deletion of Alice Davenport, are the same. What is unexplainable was Mack Riley's removal from the film.

6 Nick Cogley

"You don't have to be crazy to work here, but it helps!"

—Favorite Keystone saying

At the age of 44, Nick Cogley was the oldest actor in *The Bangville Police*. Previously seen in serials playing character roles, he then played opposite Mabel Normand, as her father, in *Hide and Seek*. His feisty quality was easily recalled by Donald Mackenzie, the director of *The Perils of Pauline*, who also doubled as "Blinky Bill, the terror of the Seven Seas."

Mackenzie told the author, who visited him in Jersey City, New Jersey:

> "Nick Cogley was middle-aged, which would have made him ineligible to play juveniles, but he was still a fearless, feisty guy.
>
> "Mack was the kind of guy who would toss everything into the pot and let things eventually work out for themselves. He certainly couldn't have done any of the stunts Pearl [White] did, but he would walk away without trying."

In *The Bangville Police*, Cogley was wisely cast as Mabel's father, a farmer who gives her a calf for a gift. Fearful that *Bangville* would be his only film, Cogley's on-the-set pratfalls were a familiar sight and cause for laughter amongst his co-workers, who were accustomed to all sorts of shenanigans on the set: spontaneous soft-shoe routines, sudden bursts into songs, etc.

According to Sennett, Cogley who had brittle bones, and never walked away from a challenge, should have used better judgment.

> "One slimy day when the pavement was slick, Mr. Cogley was egged on too far...and did a back flip which gave him a compound fracture in his left leg. We kept Mr. Cogley on the payroll, but it was a matter of pride with my comedians not to break themselves."

—Mack Sennett, *King of Comedy*

Nick Cogley's mishap was important to warrant a news article on July 19, 1914 in *The Toledo Blade*: "Nick Cogley is still on crutches from a compound fracture..."

Mabel Normand, always the prankster, decided to play a joke on the bedridden Cogley. Knowing that Cogley's wife was a terrible fanatic about cleanliness to the point that smoking was banned on the premises, and dishes were not allowed to remain in the sink after meals, she telephoned Cogley and informed him that the studio had plans to photograph his living room as a possibility for a set for an upcoming film. Knowing that Cogley's cast on his leg made him immovable, Mabel told the visiting electricians and crew where to place the lights and a dozen smudge pots for a job that would be completed in a little over an hour. Everything would be completed by the time *Mrs.* Cogley would be home, and totally unaware of what had transpired in her absence.

When Mrs. Cogley returned some *three* hours later, she found a filthy living room with smoke and an almost suffocated husband, and the Santa Monica fire department hosing down the walls!

The joke had obviously backfired, and Mabel had to shell out several thousand dollars to pay for damages and restoration.

Cogley recovered and was eventually made a director.

While he was not overly fond of what Mabel had done, she had made him aware of the Keystone style.

7 Bobby Dunn

"There were always elements in the Keystone which jeopardized its future—it lacked variety, it was often dull, its lapses of taste were serious…The ideal comedy of Mack Sennett is a fairly standardized article…They include a simple, usually preposterous plot, frequently a burlesque of a serious play; more important are the characters, grotesque in bulk, form or makeup; and finally, the events which have as little connection with the plot as, say, a clog dance in musical comedy. In the early days of the Keystone, it is said the plot was almost nonexistent in advance, and developed out of the set and the props."

—Gilbert Seldes
The Keystone the Builders Rejected

Wisconsin-born (1891) Bobby Dunn, prior to being hired as part of the *Bangville* ensemble, was never an actor who came from the world of touring stock companies. His background was the circus, where he performed as a champion high-diver with the Dr. Carver's diving horses troupe across the United States. The career came to an abrupt halt when a sudden lack of focus caused him to lose an eye.

No longer to be billed as a champion high diver, he applied for work at Keystone as a stunt man.

Upon a dare from director Henry Lehrman, Dunn ventured onto the roof of Los Angeles' Hotel Bryson and dove 85 feet into a large mortar box, emerging damage-free, and receiving a five-dollar fee.

Buster Keaton would constantly refer to him as "courageous" and "lion-hearted." Even partially sighted, he still maintained his agility. Sennett, from his height of six-four, remarked that Bobby was short, but immediately teamed him with the much taller Slim Summerville, with whom he became a lifelong friend.

Mexican revolutionary general Pancho Villa, who wanted to become a motion picture star, gave reluctant permission for the Sennett Company to film *Villa at the Movies*. While Sennett was cautious to grant Villa to appear in the film, Villa was pacified when he was told his name would be included in the title, and not in a derogatory way! He would be described as a *freedom* fighter!

With the help of trick photography, Dunn would be seen riding atop an artillery shell.

The teaming of Dunn and Summerville did not always play well on the screen. Christie comedienne Babe London, who was often described as the female Roscoe Arbuckle, offered this explanation to the author at the Actors Home Woodland Hills:

> "Bobby Dunn had a wonderful sense of humor, and with Slim Summerville they could have been a good team, but they were never given good material, good scripts to work with.
>
> "Off-camera, very funny guys who could light up a room whenever they entered. But when you have silent films, with pantomime to put your laughs across, you need a good line for audiences to follow. When you first saw them, you laughed because of their physical differences, but where do you go from there?

"There's a good reason Keystone was called The Fun Factory. A lot of jokes and funny situations occurred. Everyone was a practical joker.

"Mack liked to receive visitors and hold his writers conferences from a huge bathtub in his office. People were shocked the first time, and then they got used to it.

"But here's the Bobby Dunn story. Bobby and Slim Summerville designed a water-bath trick to play on one of their co-workers [Hale Hamilton]. They somehow managed to get a cold bucket of water between the wall and top of the door. Whoever walked into that room or office would somehow tilt the bucket of water…You know the rest

"But the person who was dosed with the water was Mack Sennett himself!"

Babe London's face reddened with laughter.

The contract of employment for Robert V. Dunn of Keystone Studios was not renewed by his own decision. Like many previous players, he chose to leave, and was immediately hired by the rival Hal Roach Studios, who had also given employment to previous Sennett players.

8 Fred Mace

"Let me tell you this: if Fred Mace had been alive at what we call the *Dawn of the American Revolution*, he, not Paul Revere, would have sounded the alarm that the British were coming. He was the unofficial Sennett scout, always on the lookout everywhere for a *face* he thought would register on camera in a crowd scene or could be developed as a possible source to be considered for a two-reeler.

"Fred Mace just knew everything that went on. He knew what *had* happened, what was *going* to happen, and what *should* have happened. He wasn't a gossip. He was a *wanderer*. When he wasn't involved in a particular scene, he would wander onto other sets, and on some days Mack would film one or two films at the same time to send out to the distributors who were always asking for a *product* to put on the screens every week.

"But Fred was always there, always watching, always aware of everything. And he wouldn't volunteer anything—unless we asked him!"

— Minta Durfee Arbuckle
Conversation with author, 1969

Dr. Fred Mace, a member of the graduating class of 1898, after a year of dental practice in Eric, Pennsylvania, decided that pulling teeth and searching for cavities were not the ways he wished to spend his life.

Just before the arrival of the twentieth century, he resolved the inner conflict (teeth versus theatre), and he decided to take the train to New York. A few weeks later, he was given a chorus-boy role in the musical *Floradora*, and he stayed with the play for the entire run. When the play went to London, he traveled with the company and remained there for the next year.

Returning to New York, he accepted roles of varying size in stock companies, which kept him touring across the United States for the next decade, save for a short time he appeared in a Bowery burlesque house, where he met Mack Sennett, with whom he appeared in an uptown house in the musical, *A Chinese Honeymoon*.

When Mack realized he will never pass a Metropolitan Opera audition, he went to work for Biograph on East 14th Street, and Mace continued to tour.

When the two men met again, almost ten years from the time they originally met, Fred had also joined Biograph, hoping to get employment in the novelty of the "flickers." With Mack, Fred Mace created "*One Round*" O'Brien, a comedy about boxing, and the *Two Sleuths*, a satire on Arthur Conan Doyle's Sherlock Holmes.

Mace, being a "theatre man," had little regard for the medium of film, but he liked the steady salary without having to subject himself to the hazards of touring. When the Keystone Company had the opportunity to go to California, Mace eagerly agreed, taking Mabel Normand and Ford Sterling. Privately, Mace was never as fond of making films as he was of the experience of doing eight shows a week on the stage.

No distrust of the camera was evident when Mace acted as the Chief of Police in *The Bangville Police*. In contrast to the other actors, Mace's work is more refined, a direct contrast to Ford Sterling's grimacing and heavy-handed mugging.

Minta Arbuckle, who knew both men, offered this comparison:

> "Ford Sterling, who regarded himself as the
> laugh king of the lot (until Charlie came

along), often played to the camera by trying to get the laughs from the people *behind* the camera and the surrounding crew.

"Was Ford Sterling funny? Yes, but his Dutch character could be a bit wearing. Fred Mace would have loved to have been the big-shot, but he was quieter. He was a doctor with a theatre background, while Ford came out of the circus, which is why Ford's playing was bigger, as if he were playing to a circus audience.

"Tents were *in the round*, while the theatres were *proscenium*. The manner of performing in a circus tent was not the same."

Mace, unlike Sterling, was a *supporting* actor at Keystone. Not a leading man. After eight months at Keystone, with popular portrayals of fat Italians and fat Spaniards, perhaps incorrect in this day, Mace, in the wake of his popularity, did the unthinkable: he asked Mack for a raise in salary.

Sennett, maintaining his constant position of *No Raises*, denied Mace's request.

Chester Conklin explained Mace's predicament.

"Mace, like the other Keystone people, was swept up in the popularity of the total group, but he was never more than one of the company. He wasn't even a second banana. Mace was a good foil, but he couldn't *carry* a picture the way Ford Sterling could.

"He came from the stage, but making movies and being onstage are two different things. The camera either loves you, or it doesn't. Mace registered well on the screen, but I always thought he wanted too much to come from too little."

Depending on who is doing the talking, the next few months in the life and career of Fred Mace were open to conjecture. That he was no longer on the Edendale lot cannot be denied.

But where did he go, and what did he do? Director Allan Dwan explained:

> "Sometimes actors, in order to save face, would leave California so they wouldn't be seen. It was a protective measure. They went to New York, or they sailed to Europe, and disappeared.
>
> "They had code words that would appear in the movie magazines to satisfy fans who wanted answers. A Tijuana vacation was really a cover-up for an abortion, and those *vacations* lasted no longer than a week. It was easier, and you avoided the press, who knew to keep away.
>
> "Don't forget the making of motion pictures was also a business. A studio can only do so much protecting, until it's time to say that so-and-so met a wonderful man or lady on a last trip somewhere, and after a *fast courtship*, she decided to *get married* and *retire*.
>
> "All very nice, respectable words for a readership that liked to feel they personally *knew* these stars. And in a way they did, because their box-office dollars established that star's longevity.
>
> "I did not know Fred Mace personally, but

he came back to California after a period of time. Nobody asked anything. *He just went away*, and came back, and Sennett took him, as he would always do when his actors did that.

"Studio heads like Sennett and Roach and Griffith believed they were like ruling emperors. They would forgive an actor's occasional indulgence, if they were still bankable. The returning actor would have to apologize privately, and sometimes eat a little crow, but most of the transgressions would be forgiven.

"Of course, the studio would be *different*. The public, in the period of their absence, sometimes *forgot* the actor, and often that actor would have to reestablish himself, often in a secondary role, but it was done. Their name might not be above the title, as it was once was, but those are the hazards of the business.

"It could happen to anyone, and often did. But they were lucky to get work. I think it was hard on the *women*. The men could get older, but the women always had to be goddesses."

Unable to accept the changing trends and shifts in audience tastes, Mace left Keystone again. It was not a smart thing to do, as Minta Arbuckle recalled.

"Mack could be forgiving, but when you leave a *second* time, that was like a slap in the face. And in this business, nobody does that to anybody.

> "Mace, at one time, was the studio scout, but he was no Mabel Normand. Even *she* knew to remain *professional* when the *personnel* was destroying her."

The theatrical season of 1917, in which Fred Mace wanted to have a significant part that would impress his colleagues at Sennett's, was already rich with the talents of Jeanne Eagels, Lenore Ulric, Helen Hayes, Katharine Cornell, Alfred Lunt, Laurette Taylor, and John and Lionel Barrymore—seasoned troupers who looked disdainfully at the burgeoning film industry. Actors, who had become indigent, worked in the motion pictures under assumed names until something better came along.

When an actor isn't seen over too long a period of time, rumors fly. *Illness? Destitute? Alcohol?*

His romance with Griffith actress Marauerite Marsh, sister of Mae Marsh, turned soured and dissolved, leaving Fred Mace by himself.

When his body was found at the Astor Hotel, Mace was only 38. Minta Arbuckle sadly remembered:

> "…that because of Fred Mace, we were hired at Keystone. Mace was always looking out for fellow actors, trying to get them jobs. In this case, the business was very cruel to him, but maybe he was cruel to *it*. You have to know your capabilities and limitations.

> "He was good to everyone but himself."

9 George Jeske

1913. The shooting of *Cohen Saves the Flag*, one of a short-lived series of what is now termed "politically incorrect" comedies, had fallen behind schedule, even though the cast included Ford Sterling (as Cohen), Mabel Normand, and Nick Cogley. Director Henry Lehrman was under double pressure—deadlines and distribution, his often-repeated phrase which he constantly told his cast.

Flag is the third in the adventures of Cohen, which featured his black derby, almost ankle-length black coat, and a dark beard. A familiar costume, until the *Flag* one-reeler placed him in Civil War surroundings, where he kept the derby and wore military gear.

Studio Vice-President Fred Balshofer daringly ordered a double firing via telephone, executed from his offices immediately—Henry Lehrman and Ford Sterling. To speed the film toward its proper deadline, he utilized outtakes that were long stored in the vault, which were usable from previous films. Only editing was required.

The problem of shooting Ford Sterling was easily resolved—shoot someone who could resemble Ford Sterling from the *back*, his *face* away from the camera.

The replacement: George Jeske.

Lehrman, whose attitude often clashed with Sennett's, particularly when he paid too much attention to Mabel Normand, was not asked to return to Keystone, while Sterling was rehired. And Jeske often doubled for him.

Away from Keystone, Lehrman, hoping to have a production company of his own, tried to hire Mabel, even giving her a larger salary than she had earned working for Mack, but it was to no avail. Mack and Mabel would have differences, but for the moment she would remain at Keystone, hoping that Mack might made a legal commitment.

Jeske, though he was one of the seven who became a Keystone Kop, was never hired as a Kop. He referred to himself:

> "...as an actor. We did everything. We handled lumber, built sets, acted, turned the camera—all for eighteen dollars a week. That was at first. When the money started rolling in, Sennett upped us. Pretty soon we were getting five dollars for an idea.
>
> "That was the birth of the gag man. Other people making pictures began paying for comedy ideas. There ought to be a gag man on every motion picture set all the time. Unless it's a heavy drama. The director is too busy to see all the opportunities. But a good gag man can sit around and watch and think."

Which is exactly what George Jeske did.
Jeske added:

> "A good gag is priceless because people remember it, and talk about it, and...word-mouth advertising is what makes it a hit."

Eventually, Jeske left the Sennett lot and went to work for Paramount, where he rose from gag man to comedy director.

Minta Arbuckle, often paired with Ford Sterling in films which were served considerably by Jeske, remarked on his departure:

> "Mack's reaction was the same—anger that they left, and sadness that somebody new will come, learn their profession, ask for a raise, and not get one. And they'll leave."

10 Hank Mann

> "Hank worked for me for eight years…When I made contracts with actors (like Hank Mann), I hired Philadelphia lawyers whose ancestors were Philadelphia lawyers to put these deals in fine print two sizes smaller and eight times as tough as the paragraphs you can't read in insurance policies."

—Mack Sennett
King of Comedy

Unlike his friend, Chester Conklin, who had a walrus mustache, Hank Mann had a mustache that resembled a push broom. Unlike the other hired candidates who walked through the front gates and were given a three-dollar-a-day contract, Hank Mann chose to leap over the fence next to the front gate. He chose a convenient time—Mack was outside.

The front fence leap was his audition piece, much in the way Roscoe executed a back flip. Cigar-chomping Sennett acted as if this behavior was the norm. After all, wasn't his studio the Fun Factory?

Twenty-six years old at the time of his hiring in 1913, Mann was fresh off the Sullivan-Considine vaudeville circuit where he worked as an acrobatic act, and also did spectacular feats of tumbling. Seemingly fearless when it came to heights, he earned a living as a sign painter and building climber.

Sennett must have sensed that Hank Mann, although quite funny, as were his pals Chester Conklin and Mack Swain, could not carry a picture in the manner of a Chaplin or Arbuckle. Yet his screen presence cannot be easily dismissed.

In trying to explain just *why* Hank Mann was so popular, Chester Conklin remarked:

> "Mack would look at somebody and in an instant just take him, or send him away, or take him as a possible crew person. Many times after someone was hired, I could see Mack thinking to himself: *Now how do I use him?*
>
> "I think the way Hank Mann just went over the fence was an attention getter. *And he certainly did get attention.* Hank Mann knew how to steal a scene, and he still remained my friend. And you weren't aware of it when he was doing it!
>
> "Hank would be sitting or standing off to one side, and then *casually* look in another direction, or he would tilt his head at an important moment and just roll his eyes for no apparent reason, or scratch his neck or straighten his eye constantly just enough to take the scene away for a split second, which on a screen can do damage.
>
> "The way he would use his eyes got laughs. He'd look like a beagle or a basset hound that was lost in the big city trying to find his way…"

Mack, knowing that Hank wasn't being used as much as his other players, would allow Hank to "job out" (accept temporary work at other studios), provided that he return.

Minta Arbuckle, who worked with Mann in the 1915 *A Bird's a Bird*, which also starred Chester Conklin, recalled:

> "...You could see Hank Mann *thinking* on camera. His gestures weren't broad like Ford Sterling. Hank Mann had the camera *listen*, if you can understand my choice of word. It was something he knew wouldn't be done if he were front and center on the screen. He'd make a small gesture, a slight wave of his hand, and he'd take the scene away. All in the name of innocence, and then he'd say to Chester, 'Did I do that?'"

Henry Lehrman, director of the L-KO comedies (Lehrman-Knock-Out Comedies), constantly used every opportunity, when he heard of Mack's personal problems, to financially lure as many of his players away from Keystone as possible.

Minta told this author:

> "From the moment I met Lehrman on the set of *Making a Living* [Chaplin's debut film, 1914], I never liked or trusted him. He was a scavenger, eyeing everything from Mack's studio operations to Mack's girl, Mabel.
>
> "It was no deep dark secret that Mack was cheap, and Lehrman's method of approach was always the same way—*more money*. It *almost* worked with Mabel when she and Mack were having one of his lack of commitment feuds when Ma was around.
>
> "But it did work with Hank Mann, Chester, and Ford Sterling. Mack was clearly upset over Hank Mann, because they were more than employer and contract player. Mann

would do anything Mack wanted him to do, but when Hank requested a raise and didn't get one, he told Mack he was going to work for Lehrman. Mack let him go, and Hank was saddened, but when the second check wasn't as big as the first check, he saw Lehrman's tricks. Lehrman liked to pick away, rather than totally destroy in one motion.

"Mack, who had started Hank at three dollars a day, was now paying him five hundred dollars a month. For Mack, this amount was staggering! What would he tell his mother?

"It must have been of some comfort that Chester and Mack Swain came back, because in their absence Mack Sennett saved on their salaries!"

For a while, all was calm. Work had resumed, and Mabel's engagement ring was back on her finger...until the problem regarding money once again reared its ugly head.

Mack's reaction was predictable. He knew how three men would react. Lehrman made another offer.

Chester Conklin left.

Mack Swain left.

Et tu, Hank Mann!

Hank had hoped that Sennett would be a little understanding, and compassionate, as the two of them often socialized after hours, but even he could see that Mann was adamant.

Not wishing to realize in 1917 that times and tastes in comedy were changing, Sennett again refused to give his loyal friend a raise. Even offering to let Hank work without a formal contract that was required of Chester and Mack Swain meant nothing. Mann clearly wanted out.

That Hank Mann's career continued well into the sound era is something none of the Keystone Players, at that moment, could predict.

Charlie Chaplin gave Hank work in three of his films—*City Lights* (1931), *Modern Times* (1936) and *The Great Dictator* (1940).

In 1917 Mack was only concerned with making the next movie, keeping Mama happy, and hoping Mabel could wait just a little while longer until, until, until…

And the Girls from Bangville

1 Dot Farley

Dot Farley, who became a member of the Keystone troupe within months of its formation, was one of the restless ones who constantly came and went as the opportunities arose: Edendale, St. Louis, Albuquerque. Many of these studios are little more than fly-by-night operations whose payrolls were sometimes never completely met, but if the actor was willing to take a chance, things would sometimes pan out.

Never a great beauty, Farley was, like Phyllis Allen and Louise Fazenda, one of the great character ladies who could be depended upon to provide solid support to the established players assuming the leads.

What was cinematically significant about *Bangville* was the hastily assembled concluding scene which paired Dot with fellow player Edgar Kennedy. They played well off each other, but it was not until the early thirties, the *sound* era, when the delightful twosome was paired together in Kennedy's *Average Man* series.

What was ironic about the career of Dot Farley was that in 1913, a year *before* she was cast in *The Bangville Police*, she was featured in *Fatty Joins the Force*, co-starring with Roscoe and Minta. Minta recalled:

> "The *Fatty* titles were an effort to showcase Roscoe and put him with as many different Keystone people as possible. I also worked with Roscoe in *Fatty's Flirtation*, which also had Hank Mann from *The Bangville Police*. Nick Cogley, also from *The Bangville Police*,

worked with Roscoe in *The Woman Haters*.

"What I'm trying to get at is that Keystone placed you with everyone in an effort to see if there was any chemistry with the players. They were one-reelers, and half-reelers.

"Dot Farley was a funny lady, and the moment you saw her you laughed. But Mack didn't know just how to use her. Mabel was a comedienne, and he built everything around her. He would have worked her to death twenty-four hours a day, seven days a week.

"Dot Farley, if you watch her later work, could hold her own. Not only as a supporting player, but as a lead. He didn't know just how to handle her. She wasn't feisty. She wanted to be busy.

"Mack would see you, then sign you, and then not know exactly what to do with you. Every decision was a gamble anyway, but his players didn't know about it, or care about it. They were on the lens side of the camera.

"Dot Farley made a few films, and *didn't* ask for a raise. When she saw there were going to be *waits* between film work, she politely told me she was going to go elsewhere, while she still had the chance of *getting* work. Any actor, then or now, will tell you—*work gets more work*.

"So she left. Without any salary, as they agreed. He didn't like what she was doing, any more than he liked what the other players did. In every case it was money, and an opportunity to make more money. If Mack didn't like to openly discuss money, his mother did!

"What did Mack think making movies was about? Other studios were experimenting with making *features*. Was Mack always going to be on page one of the industry trade papers week after week?"

2 Mabel Normand

Mabel's humor grew increasingly physical as she continued to play opposite Chaplin, and the much heavier Roscoe Arbuckle. Both Mabel and Roscoe were a striking contrast to each other. Mabel, sixty inches tall and one hundred pounds, to Roscoe's seventy inches tall and two hundred and sixty pounds, were a source of laughter the moment the camera saw them next to each other.

Sexy and full-bodied as Mabel was, Sennett trusted her with Charlie. They were buddies, but not lovers. Possibly to avoid repeated requests for higher salaries, Sennett allowed Charlie and Mabel to co-direct their films together (*Caught in a Cabaret, Her Friend the Bandit, Mabel's Busy Day, Mabel's Married Life*), and joined the two of them for *The Fatal Mallet*.

Minta continued on Sennett's delegation of directorial responsibilities:

> "Mack sensed, as Charlie and Mabel and Roscoe were becoming more popular, to allow them to direct a sequence, or even the entire film, and hopefully he wouldn't have to give them that much more money.
>
> "The origination of the pie-throwing, so often associated with Keystone, accidentally happened on the set of *Caught in a Cabaret* during a break for lunch.
>
> "Mabel was a great sport about everything

involving men. She could dish it out, as well as take it. I was on that set when one of the prop men made a playful pass at Mabel. She laughed, and reached in her box-lunch for a blueberry pie, and she hurled it at him, in an effort to make him stop trying to kiddingly grab her. He wasn't trying to touch her. It was a joke. The pie landed right smack in his face, and everybody laughed.

"Word got back to Mr. Sennett, who came down, and asked to see this repeated. It was, and he laughed, and it was used in the film. In fact, everybody used it, but the best pie battle was seen in Laurel and Hardy's *The Battle of the Century*."

June 1967. Chicago. The Playboy Theatre.
Prior to its televised showing of *The Eternal Tramp*, a documentary on Charlie Chaplin, for which the author wrote the score, Gloria Swanson, the narrator, holds an informal conference in the lobby for any and all who would listen. Gloria was an extra (the girl seated at a typewriter) in Chaplin's 1915 Essanay two-reeler, *His New Job.*

In the lobby of the theatre, Gloria Swanson is holding court. She wears a black dress, which rises well above her knee, and displays a lot of leg. She is sixty-seven, and she still has the presence to bring it off—for someone who is sixty-seven. That she wears a large diamond that is obviously not fake, the faded movie queen in *Sunset Boulevard*, her comeback film of 1950, for which she was nominated for an Oscar as Best Actress.

Even though this is supposed to be an *informal* few words, it is obvious that she is *well prepared* to be informal.

She tilts her head back in such a manner that you know a camera must be hidden and lurking somewhere.

She delicately raises her right hand and gestures for silence. Like obedient schoolchildren, everyone is silent. And respectful.

"Mack Sennett thought I could be another Mabel Normand, if I stayed around. Mabel was a lovely, talented, *troubled*, funny girl. She was having problems with Mack, and I was having problems of my own with Wally at the same time. [Husband Wallace Beery, with whom she co-starred in Sennett's 1916 *Teddy at the Throttle* during her pudding-face period.] Staying with Sennett would have made me a *Mabel* substitute, and staying with Wally...He was one mistake I only made once. Mack was overly possessive. I hate men like that. But Mabel stayed and took it, thinking Mack would change. But she was wrong. She was very wrong. You can't change men. Men are what they are: men.

"Mabel could have had any man she wanted, but what she would have with Mack, what I had with Wally, is the same no-win situation.

"I don't think Mack was the marrying kind—especially with his mother looming in the background watching everything he did until Mabel's pressure put Mama in the foreground. Mabel made too many personal concessions, and that cost her her personal integrity and identity. She was afraid she'd lose her job. Ultimately, when anyone enters this unpredictable profession, one must, in order to survive, be able to make a living.

"Fortunately, I've been able to do that. And that's why we're here: to see each other, and go on with our lives. Thank you."

Mack and Mabel

Chapter 1
Walk East on 14th

Come home, come home!
Catherine Sinnott
Letters to her son, Mack Sennett

Home. What was *home* to someone who willingly walked away from his family to seek his fortune in an unknown field?
 A theatre was *home*.
 A vaudeville stage was *home*.
 A burlesque house was *home*.

1908. Mack Sennett did not go into moviemaking as his first choice of career. He was a failed stage actor, perpetually forced to tour with stock companies across the United States, barely eking out a living, and in constant fear of shoddy producers abandoning the company in small towns.
 He had a passable chorus boy voice, and had studied with a *Signor* Fontanan at the urging of Catherine, his mother, who wanted him to have a life of respect: singing at New York's Metropolitan Opera.
 His father, a boilermaker, wanted his son to remain at home in Richmond, Quebec and work in a factory. A voice was something nice to hear in a Sunday Mass, which would make the family very proud. Not in a theatre.
 A *career in* New York City? That *Godless* place?
 His New York City debut in 1902, when he was 22, did not occur at the much desired Metropolitan Opera House.
 He made his debut as the rear end of a horse at a Bowery Burlesque

house, whose headliner was the notorious Little Egypt, a favorite since the Chicago World's Fair of 1893.

Mack need not have worried about scandal. Little Egypt's bumps and grinds had seen younger, more publicity-getting better days. The circuit was still flourishing, but Little Egypt was now an *old* veteran, whose audiences knew what to expect, and had probably seen the act before when they were both in better financial circumstances.

Still, for Mack, it was working with a "name," and experience was *experience*. He did not tell his mother, and his debut story was, years later, a good story to tell at parties.

Parties or no, his career did not seem to go in any direction. He regularly answered his mother's *Come home, come home* letters, which always included a twenty-dollar bill, as an inducement, supporting his "free" time.

Like other struggling actors, he lived in rooming houses in New York's red brick district, often described very realistically in O. Henry newspaper short stories. Often other struggling actors sneaked in at night, slept on the floor, and somehow managed to bathe before leaving before the sun rose.

Wisely, Mack kept his name in the mind of burlesque impresario Frank Sheridan, whose wheels traveled along the Eastern seaboard, and often went to Chicago. To his constantly questioning mother, Mack was "on the road, singing in shows," he *always* would sing in a Catholic choir whenever possible.

Singing in a Catholic Church choir was a great source of pride to Mrs. Sinnott, as it meant that even in the corrupt world he was able to keep up his spirituality.

Choir singing, every musical actor knew, paid little money, but it did have rewards. Often congregants fed the singers, and some would let them have a room.

Returning to New York, Mack made his legitimate debut in Raymond Hitchcock's musical, *King Dodo*. Although his name was not specifically singled out for praise, employment in the succeeding *A Chinese Honeymoon, Wang!*, and *Piff! Paff!! Pouf!!* followed. The New York theatre was fascinated with Asian themes. One of the popular straight plays was *East Is West,* which starred Fay Bainter.

That Mack was *somewhat* steadily working in the New York theatre and receiving paychecks wasn't *totally* satisfying to his mother, nor her boilermaker factory husband, on whom Mack turned his back and abandoned his family.

A *true* success, in Mrs. Sinnott's terms, meant singing at the Metropolitan Opera. At the opera, audiences attended in tuxedos and women were dressed in fine gowns and wore expensive jewelry.

What did the audience wear at the Bowery burlesque house, Mack must have asked himself, after reading her letters and accepting her twenty-dollar bills. Until the New York runs of the three Asian plays stopped, his letters were becoming reticent on the matters of employment.

On 7th Avenue, between 41st and 42nd Streets, Sennett and other actors who were "between shows" were able to exist on one meal a day—the *free* lunch of ham, cheese and bread which was always available during the lunch hour. A schooner of beer was a nickel and it only cost a nickel.

A well-timed lunch and a few schooners of nickels were all that was necessary to keep Brady's in business. Actor-patrons learned what straight plays were going on tour, what musicals needed replacements, and what Midwestern stock companies needed chorus people at the last minute.

Brady's was not only a source of professional tips; it was a source of rising or falling reputations. Who was difficult, who was respected. Mack always knew he could always find employment on the burlesque wheels, and he also knew when it was more advantageous to remain in New York, and tell his inquiring mother that he was in demand with opportunities to perform at Irish wakes and funerals with The Cloverdale Boys, a hastily-formed group that worked the banquet circuit for nothing and earned a nice sum for singing at wakes. Songs about dearly departed mothers, sung at the appropriate time, always guaranteed a heavier tip when the hat was passed around.

Taking advantage of the recently created subway system, there were no real transportation problems, and the group was in demand in New York, Brooklyn and the Bronx.

Being hired as part of the chorus for Victor Herbert's musical *Mlle. Modiste*, starring Fritzi Scheff, was a mixed blessing. Best known for the successful *Babes in Toyland* (1903), the *Modiste* producers chose December 25 to be the Opening Night.

Fritzi Scheff, whose only competition was Maude Adams, who had just completed a run in James M. Barrie's *The Little Minister* and wasn't going into her next play, *Peter Pan*, until February, had virtually handed the season over to Fritzi, whose new song, "Kiss Me Again," was going to be an American standard, and one of Herbert's greatest hits.

Mlle. Modiste was a solid New York hit, playing an initial run of 205 performances. Fritzi Scheff was now firmly established, and she remained in the musical through 1906 and 1907, reviving the musical in 1913 and 1929 for newer audiences.

While Mack's mother was pleased, *Mlle. Modiste* was a golden opportunity for her son to make a transition to the Metropolitan Opera. It seemed only logical. Mack had been doing chorus work in a few musicals and singing in the chorus of a few church choirs over the years.

Would Miss Scheff make it possible for Mack to audition for the Met?

Wasn't Miss Scheff aware of his voice and the fact that he, like Miss Scheff, had been doing eight shows a week? And never missing a single performance, despite all kinds of weather?

Most important—did Miss Scheff *like* his work? Did she like *him*?

Mack knew better than to present Fritzi Scheff with his mother's lines of justification. He also knew, after all of this time in New York, that he owed his mother something for all of those unreturned twenty-dollar bills she had been sending him...

Fritzi Scheff, always kind to her supporting casts, and fully aware how difficult it was to make a transition from grand opera to musical comedy, was sympathetic to Mack. He was always respectful, and she had known there was little *emotional* support from his mother. Indeed, the leads in many plays were aware that a good leading person looks better when the supporting cast *really* supports you. Many leading performers originally started as chorus people and members of supporting casts.

Some never forget...

Fritzi Scheff approached Frank Damrosch, one of the Metropolitan Opera scouts, telling him of Mack's chorus work in *Mlle. Modiste*, briefly telling him of Mack's previous stage experience.

Would he listen to him one afternoon in his office?

Damrosch's appraisal was honest and frank.

Mack, like most concert-trained Broadway chorus singers, was certainly capable of sustaining a perfectly respectable career in the Broadway theatre as a Broadway chorus singer in support of the leading man or lady. With *luck*, he might secure a leading role in a touring *stock* company of a musical, but he was *not*, under any circumstances, a singer of Metropolitan Opera capability or quality.

What Mack had been anticipating had finally been spoken. His *mother's* operatic wishes did not become his ambitions after trying to establish himself as *anything* in New York.

There was always the burlesque wheel, but how long could he last, in any city, before the Law crafted a performance, arrested him along with the headliner, and put the company in jail.

He had been lucky in his tours with Sheridan's company. There had been threats and warnings, but no arrests, and no newspaper publicity.

What could he tell the theatrical managers in New York?

Most important—would could he tell his *mother*?

Mack had returned to the routine of lunches at Brady's, trying to find available floor space in the red brick district. Although he wanted to send some of his mother's money back to her, he did not want to create the illusion that he was that much of a Broadway success. She certainly was aware that her opera ambitions did not bear fruit, and she was aware that he was going into another play.

What neither Catherine nor Mack knew was that *The Boys Company of B* was going to be his last play in New York.

Shavian actor Arnold Daly had scored a personal success as Marchbanks in the original (1903) New York production of George Bernard Shaw's *Candida*, playing opposite Dorothy Donnelly in the title role.

Having established Shaw on Broadway in three more Shaw works (*You Never Can Tell, John Bull's Other Island* and *The Man of Destiny*), he was arrested in the course of the run of Shaw's scandalous *Mrs. Warren's Profession*, on the grounds that it was an immoral play. Both Daly and his leading lady Mary Shaw (no relation to the playwright) were brought to trial and quickly released.

For a while, there were no more Shaw plays with Arnold Daly.

Eager to distance himself, Daly went into *The Boys of Company B*. Daly's role would be replaced by John Barrymore in his theatrical debut.

For the duration of the run, one of the *Boys* was played by Mack Sennett.

Although he was billed as 14th in the *Playbill*, it was time for Sennett to take stock of himself. While his contemporaries had packed their valises and left their Hell's Kitchen furnished rooms, he didn't want to give up and return home to face a never encouraging family who thought he was wrong for leaving in the first place.

He was faced with two solutions: to return home or to look for other venues.

Although he had ignored it since its beginnings downtown, a new novelty was making its presence known on 14th Street. Storefronts were becoming theatres, theatres that showed *moving* pictures on a blank wall. Former vaudeville theatres were being replaced with *Nickelodeons*.

The price of admission to these wooden bridge chair auditoriums was well within everyone's affordability—one nickel. Five cents.

These motion picture novelties were made by studios. Some were in the immediate neighborhood!

You only had to walk east on Fourteenth.

Chapter 2
The Hidden World Beneath the Street

"I bumbled my way into motion pictures."

—Mack Sennett
King of Comedy

Although the earliest attempts at motion pictures were first exhibited in New York in 1895, it was *The Great Train Robbery* (1903), an Edison project, which made people take notice of an emerging art form.

It told a story in pictures, and without spoken dialogue. The final image, the aiming and firing of a gun at its audiences, caused screams of surprise, and sent some of them running out of the theatres.

Although the legitimate stage actors dismissed this new entertainment as something for immigrants who could not speak English or read the titles on the outside posters, shrewd producers saw the "flickers" as something that would be more popular than the Sunday comic strips.

When an unemployed Sennett decided in 1908 to walk to 11 East 14th Street to investigate, he became aware that the city was changing. The turn-of-the-century pushcarts with their competing prices were still there, but the storefront nickelodeons with their inexpensive prices of admission were steadily attracting more patrons right from the sidewalk who were willing to pay the cheap prices of admission for a few minutes of entertainment.

That new studios were springing up in Brooklyn, Fort Lee, and even in a loft on West 24th Street, was of little importance. They simply wanted a product, which meant a reel a week, in order to meet competitive demands.

Biograph, located at 11 East 14th, was Mack's final destination. The studio, he had heard from drinkers at the bar at Brady's, was having hard times. Lack of material, lack of actors.

If you wanted employment, and you had that "look" that registered on camera, you were assured of employment. The salary was five dollars a day, and there was no need to worry. Nobody received on-screen billing. Five dollars a day and a box lunch were enough to sustain any actor until the next theatre job came.

Many at Biograph had theatre experience. Being "high-hat" had no place. Everyone was in the same boat—out of work.

The advantage of "flickers," Mack remembered from talking to the actors at Brady's, was that they could be shown over and over again, from morning until evening. There would always be a steady stream of customers.

There were more than 10,000 nickelodeons across the United States.

Unlike the theatre, whose prices were high and whose plays had short runs and had artistic temperaments to deal with, "flickers" were easy and quick to make. No spoken dialogue to worry about. You only had to use your *face*, and know how to indicate by gestures—*happy, sad, anticipation, jealousy*. And use those gestures in the story *at the right time*. Unlike the theatre, where every performance in front of an audience was non-stop, an actor could repeat the sequence again. A film editor could fix everything.

The *director* only had to keep the motion going.

A *stage* director, a *film* director.

Biograph, once Mack found the *location*, had no outside sign of identification. The studio had a brownstone of the 1850s—four stories with a commercial basement that opened onto the street. Originally tenanted by the Steck Piano Company, Steck vacated the premises. The basement stores were rented and the building was leased to Biograph for five thousand dollars.

Wisely, nothing was easily identifiable from the outside, if you were just passing by. How many times had Mack walked past this location without bothering to look?

The basement store was a rented tailor's shop. Nobody knew

what was happening in the back rooms, or the rooms on the upstairs floors. This was a studio, not a brothel! It was not a waterfront tavern where drunken customers rewarded the effort of the singer with a few tossed pennies!

The Biograph Studio day, Sennett would learn, ended when it was deemed okay. A reel (ten to twelve minutes) a week had to be ready for the theatres. Seven days a week. Year in and year out. At five dollars a day. Plus a box lunch.

George ("Old Man") McCutcheon, the president of the studio, handled the directing, although he was not always in good health due to a bad heart. He had an office that was accessible after descending a half flight from the street, then going through the double doors, and then up another set of stairs to the main floor. The excessive climbing ultimately was discouraging. By the time his office was finally reached, the complainer was too breathless to speak!

George, aware of Biograph's declining fortunes, surrendered his office to his son, Wallace, who wanted no part of the studio, preferring to pursue a career in musical comedy. He was the oldest of George's seven children, and had little say in the matter. Motion picture studios were family businesses, and often saw the patriarch saw himself as the founder of a dynasty, be it in the "flickers" or the corporate world.

George's seven children were employed in some capacity at the studio. Son Wallace married Pearl White, the heroine of the serial, *The Perils of Pauline.*

Wallace McCutcheon also hired Mack Sennett. In what capacity Mack was going to function, Mack did not know.

He knew he was going to work in the hidden world beneath the street. Whatever job he would be given an early opportunity for self-publicity.

Chapter 3
At Biograph–First Days, First Impressions

> "Everything in the arts is a matter of timing. Being there at the right time when they need you. Having just what they want, and knowing how to sell it.
>
> "Acting is the least of it. They will tell you exactly what to do."

—Anita Loos, Biograph screenwriter
Conversation with author, May 1972

When Mack was asked at the foyer window at Biograph what he could do, he immediately thought of his debut in the Bowery burlesque as the rear end of the horse a few years ago.

His answer was short and succinct. "Anything."

Seeing the broad-shouldered, thirty-eight-year-old in his bulldog shoes, and his no-neck, large head, the big guy resembled a box. If he could act, that was a bonus.

For this moment in time, the studio needed big guys who could be useful at handling props or packaging film for distribution. Mack was an all-purpose muscle man, who could lug the sets when they had to be in the right direction of the sun for outdoor scenes. It was a seven-day work week whose specific hours varied with each day. Some days were easier than others, but he knew to expect that. In the legitimate theatre there were no unions or labor organizations, and it was the same for the actors as the technicians. With nickelodeons showing one-reelers twelve hours a day, there was more than enough justification for Biograph and the other studios to complete a reel a week and to keep the product coming for the always constant customers who wanted full value for their nickel. Something new, something different, but with the same actors who were audience-pleasers.

On the set and in the Biograph studio, Griffith wouldn't allow the use of the word "flickers" to be used in connection with the work they were doing. If the films were shot and hand cranked at a correct speed, the audience wouldn't laugh unnecessarily at the wrong time. If the projectionist was drunk and hand cranked the one-reeler before an audience without any effort to watch the screen at the same time, the flow of the action would mar the success of the presentation.

The Biograph, Mack soon realized, had to surpass its competitors in order to survive, and it had to function together as one person—D.W. Griffith.

Like Mack, who followed Griffith everywhere and was like a shadow, Griffith was *also* a failed writer and actor who had done his share of tours and stock across the country. Approximately five years older than Mack, Griffith, unbeknownst to a majority of those at Biograph, also had a wife, Linda Arvidson, who occasionally worked at the studio. She, too, when a body was needed to fill the scene, would take her place with the rest of the actors in front of the camera.

Mack's muscle man talents eventually landed an on-camera role as one of the hicks in *Balked at the Altar*. He was relegated to the background—in an obvious effort to be seen, he waved his arms, much as the young John Wayne did, many years later, when he was an extra in John Ford's silent *Hangman's House* in a sequence filmed at a racetrack. Wayne also waved his arms and whooped it up as his horse rode into victory.

While Sennett's initial screen performance did not single him out for any performance kudos, his off-camera clowning was certainly noticed and noted by his co-workers when he returned to doing crew work for other films, prior to being utilized in completely different roles: *Betrayed by a Handprint* (a butler), *Father Gets into the Game* (the head of the family), *Mr. Jones at the Ball* (a partygoer).

As Sennett's film work increased, he found himself in contact with more of the players in different shooting locations as part of the action, and in less demand as a member of the crew. A good many of the Biograph men, in order to speed things along and because they were reporting to the studio seven days a week, often participated in crew work, when the occasion so warranted.

Blanche Sweet, who had recently signed with Biograph, remembered Sennett as:

> "A very brash, vulgar man with horrible manners. He certainly wasn't any sort of gentleman. Luckily for me, I didn't have to be around him and when I was, I did my best to keep distance between us. As much distance as possible without being very obvious about it.
>
> "Mr. Griffith was very respectful to the ladies. A very courtly, refined gentleman in the Southern manner. At the end of the day's shooting, he would wish us a good evening, and sometimes he would bow, always showing breeding and behave like a colonel or general in the War Between the States! Those kinds of manners, if you know what I mean. He was very grand and mannered in a Southern way.
>
> "*But Mack Sennett*! He would think nothing of spitting out that tobacco he'd been chewing all day without even bothering to stop to take a breath. That man didn't even think enough to look and see if there were any spittoons in the area! He would just spit without warning, and whoever was near would have to jump away!
>
> "I'm happy I never had to work with him.

Neither did Dorothy nor Lillian. But Mary [Pickford] did!"

Weeks into his employment at Biograph, Sennett was aware that professional advancement might depend on availability, and *being seen* at the beginning and at the end of the working day by the boss was always interpreted as a sign of dedication to one's work, and an opportunity to receive private lessons from the Master.

Griffith would discuss possible new camera angles he might use to sustain audience interest and involvement, possible classics he could adapt without paying any royalties, and what would be shot on the next working day.

Just by coincidence Griffith would run into Sennett at the corner of his apartment building on East 37th Street or at the Claridge Hotel on Broadway and 44th Street, a noticeable indication that the financial situations of Mr. Griffith and the studio had improved.

As writers for this newly evolving medium, both men could freely discuss literary construction problems, occasionally reminding each other that, despite their age differences, both had similar experiences in the theatre and on the road. Though their personal philosophies and attitudes clashed during some of these impromptu walks, Sennett still saw Griffith as a person who was revolutionizing the industry.

For the moment, the policeman was an authority of the Law, and worthy of every respect. That these authorities of the Law would be a subject of ridicule in two years (1911) was a personal thought Sennett would keep in abeyance.

He still had many things to learn.

While Mack's raucous behavior and tobacco-spitting had been repulsive to many of his female co-workers, most notably Blanche Sweet, he did have a staunch defender in Linda Arvidson, Mrs. D.W. Griffith. Mack's constant high spirits and humor, she felt, should be put on the screen.

The Curtain Pole, based on a concept by Griffith cameraman Billy Bitzer, provided Mack with a significant leading role, although Griffith was very reluctant to construct a film about the problems of installing a curtain pole. There was nothing inherently funny about the subject, although he believed humor should come from the situation and not from just running around and acting simple.

But Linda Arvidson's pressure prevailed and *The Curtain Pole*, with Linda Arvidson as the leading lady, was filmed in Fort Lee, New Jersey and not released until the completion and testing of *Those Awful Hats*, a half-reeler where Sennett's character, a silly Frenchman named Monsieur Dupont, was tested in a showing before an audience at New York's Union Square Theatre.

Art is art, but business, an experience D.W. Griffith knew, was always business. *The Curtain Pole*, while not a career maker for Mack Sennett the actor, was a crowd pleaser and made money.

What was quite unexpected occurred during the filming—the curtain pole, the *actual* curtain pole used in the film fell on Linda Arvidson's head, knocking her unconscious.

Mr. Griffith decided to discontinue any plans for making Mack's Monsieur Dupont character a continuing series. The matter of the accident was something unspoken between the two men during the mornings and evenings of their walks, but Mack deemed it wise to pay an occasional house visit on his own.

Co-star or no, Linda Arvidson was the boss's wife, even though it was believed to be a well-kept secret.

The new arrival from Toronto, where she was born Mary Smith, walked up to the foyer window at the age of sixteen, announcing who she was with great confidence that belied her age.

Mary Pickford.

As was proper, her mother (Charlotte) was at her side, acting as her protector. She needn't have been, for eleven years of touring in plays across the United States, beginning in Toronto, made Mary a seasoned trouper with a seasoned eye and the common sense to say exactly what she wanted. At the age of twelve, she was earning forty dollars a week and supporting her family.

At the Biograph foyer window, she demanded a salary of *ten* dollars a day, rather than the standard five dollars given to the rest of the players.

Mary's request was granted—ten dollars a day.

She didn't need her mother to protect her, but her mother was a constant convenience when she had to speak to those in charge when her demands weren't met.

Mack met Mary on the set of *The Violin-Maker of Cremona*. Filmed in two days, Mary played an Italian girl who is the subject of a competition for her hand between violin-makers.

Although Mack was once again consigned to a very minor role, he saw this as another opportunity. He could watch Mary without her being aware of it. *The Violin-Maker* was only her second film. In her debut film, *Her First Biscuits*, a seven-minute split-reel, her greatest fear wasn't her acting (she had eleven years of theatrical experience), but being *seen* walking into the Biograph studio. People *of the theatre* did not view the "flickers" with much respect. It was a sign of hard times.

Mary's worries were short-lived. The camera loved her, and she loved the money she was getting.

Always kind to her co-workers in front of, and behind, the camera, Mary was very approachable to anyone with possibilities for films. New scripts were always read. A studio like Biograph operated like a repertory theatre. There were no favorites. A lead in one film could become one of the crowd for the next. It was the final collective product that mattered, and the reactions of the audience that determined the success of a film. They were paying the admission at the nickelodeons.

Mack's initial submission, Mary felt, seemed too close to the O. Henry stories she had read in *Munsey's* and the *World*, who regularly published his submissions.

While *The Curtain Pole* was an effort his mother could see, she still continued to urge her errant, dream-chasing son to come home.

> "We are all proud of your wonderful success.
> Have you paid your room rent?"

While Mack was earning a steady salary, his career hadn't progressed in any noticeable direction. He was still living in a single and conveniently waiting to catch his mentor going to or from Biograph.

And always there were questions…

Sennett began to wonder. Was Griffith's ensuing success in a medium more popular with illiterates with limited incomes than with the wealthier intelligentsia going to prevent his work from being seriously considered as something of worth?

Following *A Convict's Stripes*, in which he played a prison guard, Sennett, in need of money, but not wanting to tell his mother of his financial straits, poured through newspapers, hoping to find something which he could fashion into a vehicle for Mary Pickford.

Although some claim *The Lonely Villa* was adapted from a newspaper article, and showed some similarity to *At the Telephone*, a play by Andre deLorde, Sennett received credit as the writer for Mary's third film.

The audiences saw Mary in what would be her trademark—fluffy blonde curls, a smile, and a real bounce to her walk. That Linda Arvidson was able to convince her husband to take twenty dollars from the studio, *which he did*, to place Mary in a "smart pale blue linen frock, blue silk stockings to match, and patent leather pumps" without any question, was further proof that D.W. and Linda believed in the potential Mary for success.

It was perfect timing—a melodrama about a family in peril for their lives. Two children and their mother are trapped in their house by robbers. What adds to the mounting of the suspense is Griffith's new innovation: cross-cutting, the switching of points of view as the husband tries to drive to where his family is imprisoned. By changing the time spent on each shot, and the addition of the drawbridge, and whether it will be raised or lowered, only heightens the effect.

With the disappearances of the nickelodeons that were suddenly being regarded as relics of the past, and the growing proliferation of storefronts being turned into makeshift movie theatres, the medium, under the direction and planning of D.W. Griffith, began to sprout wings. Audiences wanted to know more about what they were seeing. What were the names of these people? Where did they come from? What have they done?

Mack kept asking questions, and waiting for the time he could develop his gags and comic situations.

Griffith, Sennett realized, had no real sense of humor, but Sennett knew that he was learning the importance of *structure*, which was important in comedy and drama.

Drama is tough. Comedy is tougher.

Everything depends on timing, and the timing for Mack Sennett was about to make itself known.

It only required being ready.

There was timing, too...

Chapter 4
In the Shadow of the Sorcerer

"I looked Hollywood over (1910), and didn't want to buy it."

—Mack Sennett
King of Comedy

Occasionally, the nickname Mack's co-workers would call him behind his back would reach him—*Griffith's Shadow*. It grew out of their constant walks, which were a subject of conversation and speculation.

Griffith they knew was married, and his wife stayed out of his way on the set when they were both there. Mack, to the best of anyone's knowledge, was never seen with any *girl*. True, he was always cordial and friendly and professional, but his habit of constantly spitting chewing tobacco did not endear him to any of the ladies, although he thought he was just "one of the boys" when he had these sudden unannounced urges to expurgate.

So long as the front office and Griffith were happy, Mack was satisfied. All that mattered were deadlines—were they met? Did the audience like what was on the screen?

Griffith was aware that while he and Mack differed on the type of subject matter being projected, and its suitability for audiences, what was important, ultimately, were the lessons Griffith was teaching. Mack was the ever-constant pupil and he observed that Griffith engendered loyalty from his actors and crew by always thanking them at the end of the day.

Griffith, who had formerly had a room in a tiny East 37th Street apartment with Linda, was now sharing a *suite* with her at the midtown Claridge Hotel in the theatre district. Living in the theatre district fed his desires to be a Broadway playwright. Having directed over two hundred films was certainly a good reason to pursue his *theatrical* ambitions, which were always of prime importance.

But could he walk away from the money he was earning as a film director and writer? He certainly was aware that more film studios were coming to New York, and the film industry in Fort Lee was blossoming.

Westerns were being filmed in the mountains of Cuddebackville, New York, a few miles away, and in Bayonne, New Jersey. There was also the constant harassment from Edison's employees in West Orange, who were raiding studios who would not use Edison film stock. Although Edison and Griffith were on good terms, Griffith, on a suggestion from Selig, decided to go to California.

There were advantages in California: distance from the East, constant sunlight, and an opportunity to use actors who did not want to work in the New York theatre. Housing was cheap, if you did not wish to live in a hotel.

True, there was a strong prejudice in certain areas whose inhabitants saw nothing wrong with blatantly stating on their signs on the front lawn—*No dogs, No Jews, and No Actors,* but that would come to change someday…

Mack's mother's constant *Come home, come home, come home* letters showed signs of stopping, and sometimes she enclosed a twenty-dollar bill to be used toward the train fare. Mack wrote a kind letter of thanks…and promptly applied the money toward his rent.

There are no records of Mrs. Sinnott threatening to come to New York for a surprise visit.

Catherine Sinnott was aware of her son's impending trip to California with approximately two dozen members of the company, including Mary Pickford and *her mother,* her brother Jack, and recent husband, Owen Moore, with whom she had eloped to Jersey City a few weeks earlier.

Mary always knew, Griffith discovered, how to *protect* herself if there were any mishaps. Chaperones were always necessary even if one happened to be her husband.

Heaven will protect the working girl, but a strong, demanding mother, an obedient brother, and a subservient were always extra assurance.

What Mack purposely neglected to tell *his* mother was that he met someone, a *girl*, who was one of the crowd of extras looking for a job.

Then he realized that *Mabel Normand* was *not* going to California with the company. Griffith didn't select her. She would remain in New York, make some money posing as an artist's model, and get some extra work at Vitagraph in Brooklyn. She had been doing extra work.

Certainly, Mabel's friendship with Mack was nothing more than that—a *friendship*.

There was no need to *alarm* his mother. She might show up unexpectedly...Maybe Mabel would remember Mack when the company returned. Just maybe...

And then he might *possibly* tell his mother about her.

Chapter 5
Simply Mabel

"As beautiful as a spring morning."

—Mack Sennett
King of Comedy

Always possessing a sense of humor about herself in her relationships, professional and non-professional, throughout her life, Mabel Normand would constantly reinvent herself when the occasion required it. She set out for New York City as a typical sixteen-year-old who believed good fortune and success were around the corner. To interviewers, the corner might have been in Boston or Providence or Staten Island, or New York itself.

Another tale she told was that she was the daughter of poor immigrants trying to survive in the vicinity of Sheepshead Bay near the docks. Because she was such a good swimmer, seeing Mabel in the water in the early hours of the daylight was a common occurrence.

What was unusual about the early morning swims, she always added, was the presence of the same dolphin that would wait for her and swim at her side!

Hearst columnist Adela Rogers St. John, sometimes called The Mother Confessor of Hollywood, told this writer:

> "*Swimming with dolphins* was a frequently told tale of Mabel's when asked to describe her life in New York before she came to California in the early days. Whether it was

true or not, everybody loved Mabel because she had a good sense of humor. Her publicity always called her 'fun-loving Mabel.'

> "Away from those publicity machines, she was one of the saddest little girls I ever knew. Just look closely at those big, beautiful dark eyes…"

Like other adolescent girls, Mabel loved going to "the pictures," but she had no great urgency to become one of the heroines she saw on the nickelodeon screens. Unlike Mary Pickford, whom she idolized and later would see at Biograph and appear with in *The Mender of Nets* (1912), Mabel was fully aware of her limitations. Mary had stage and vocal training and touring experience.

Mary, with her blue eyes and long golden curls, was the picture of angelic innocence. Mabel was also quite capable of holding up a production's shoot if things were not going her way or to her satisfaction. With or without her mother, Mary knew how to fight for what she wanted. Men were afraid of her. Mary knew how to navigate her way through the machinations of the *business* of making movies.

Mabel never thought of *making* movies. She only thought of *going* to the movies, and trying to see every Mary Pickford release. Sometimes more than once.

In 1909 Mabel was a three-dollar-a-day New York model who posed for photographers. She modeled frocks and evening gowns. She knew that *lingerie* paid more money than holding umbrellas or flowers, but there was always one's reputation to think about. *Lingerie* ladies were always subjected to rumors of impropriety and becoming known as fast and loose.

Reputation or no, impropriety or no, being fast and loose—these words and privately whispered phrases meant nothing. The Arts and people in the Arts were always subject to scrutiny. What does anybody really know about the Mona Lisa?

Frocks or flowers, she knew frocks paid more, and she had nobody to support her. Heaven will protect the working girl. Modeling frocks paid considerably more than modeling patterns at fifty cents an hour for *Delinator* magazine, and she knew she might meet men who might help her…

Mabel constantly assured her cautious, over-protective mother that she would never be kidnapped on the evil subways, and licentious men would not kidnap her on the Staten Island Ferry and deliver her into the hands of white slavers who would bound and gag her and ship her to an evil place, never to be seen again on *The Way of All Flesh*!

Mabel, sometimes believing the warnings of her mother, *walked* from the Battery to midtown Manhattan to make herself available to commercial artists Charles Dana Gibson, James Montgomery Flagg and the Leyendecker brothers who put her on the covers of *The Saturday Evening Post* and *Life* magazines. She also was pictured next to the new favorable soft drink of the day—Coca-Cola!

Actress Alice Joyce, in her early days, was a model employed at the Kalem Studios at 131 West 24th Street in the Chelsea district, and suggested Mabel go to Biograph on her free time and present herself at the foyer window as someone who could be used as a day-player.

Biograph paid five dollars a day, and there was always the possibility of overtime which could go as late as eleven o'clock. Besides hiring actors, there was the chance of working in the wardrobe department as a seamstress. The money wasn't as lucrative, but it would be enough to tide her over until something important came along. And there were always *meals*.

On the day Mabel reported at Biograph, she learned that extras were needed to be used in crowds at the train station and guests at a society dinner to be utilized on the following day. Men had to provide their own tuxedos, ladies their own gowns. Report tomorrow at seven a.m.

Truth or cinema lore, Mack and Mabel may have passed each other in the corridors. Neither said anything to each other.

Wilfred Lucas, the assistant to D.W. Griffith, noticing Mabel's legs, immediately fitted her in a page's costume, instructing her to stand behind the Queen and carry her train.

Do you have anything planned for the day? Could you start now?

While they were shooting, sixteen-year-old Mabel could not help but notice the constant leering of a "stocky red-faced Irishman" who kept his eyes constantly on her legs that were covered with black tights. She had never experienced this when she was posing for the artists in midtown Manhattan. A few winks and stares were to be expected, but this man kept staring in front of everyone on the set. Was it always going to be like this every day?

The man who maintained the same spot close to the cameraman, she learned, was thirty-four years old. He was *eighteen* years older! Was there nobody there to tell him to go away and leave her alone? He was a distraction. Was this what she had been warned about?

His name was Mack Sennett, and when he introduced himself to Mabel, he said he was Mr. Griffith's *assistant* and one day he might have his own company, and he would be directing her at a larger salary—*one hundred and twenty-five dollars a week!*

The thought of sudden big money from a total stranger made her laugh. He sounded like the commissioned portrait painters who offered extra money for "private sessions" after business hours.

The bell rang. She left him standing there. It was time for lunch. Stardom could come later. It was time to eat, and she was hungry.

Dazed by the audacity of this "Mad Irishman's" offer, she still daydreamed her way through lunch until the ringing of the bell told her it was time to work. The red-faced stocky Irishman who had bothered her earlier did not give any further instructions for the afternoon's work. Mabel assumed that the shoot had been finished.

Mr. Lucas directed Mabel to another part of the studio, where she was outfitted in another costume, one she would never have in her own possession, and shown where this new shoot would be taking place. She couldn't get over her good luck. On her first day of work, two extra jobs, and she would be earning ten dollars. Would there be more opportunities like this?

Suddenly she realized the thought of the subways or even the Staten Island Ferry no longer scared her. Millions of people use both modes of transportation everyday. She never heard of any strange incidents. At least she knew who to be careful of—a thirty-four-year-old stocky, red-faced Irishman who kept leering at her. He wouldn't dare leer at her in full view of the public. He would be arrested!

Mabel returned to modeling, unaware of what she had done. The ten dollars she received must have meant everything had gone smoothly. The ten-dollar bill in her purse was proof of that. The deadline was met. One reel a week. Right on time for the nickelodeons.

Weeks into her employment as a model, Mack and Mabel had a chance encounter in the Times Square area. She was on her way to the offices of one of the magazine illustrations, while he was going to one of the vaudeville theatres to watch one of the performers.

That Mack was angry was no surprise. Didn't she pay him no attention that first day she reported to Biograph? Wasn't she paid for *two* shoots instead of one?

Whose fault was it that she was taken from one shoot to another without any explanation?

Was that why they weren't calling her?

Who had a bigger right to be angry?

In her mind she believed she was right not to go back to 14th Street and the studio with the hidden entrance. Legitimate theatres and burlesque houses were out in full view. Why were the newspapers editorializing that the nickelodeons were contributing to the degradation of the community, and the darkened parlors, which operated twelve hours a day, were centers of sinful behavior?

For Mack, Mabel's arguments were almost a replay of his own mother's tirades. But was Mabel speaking for herself or for her mother? Were the movies the work of the devil?

Then why did Mrs. Normand accept ten dollars of the devil's money?

When Mabel realized that the money she earned for a day's work at Vitagraph was more than she had earned posing for the mid-town artists, she swallowed her pride and returned to Biograph, hoping she would be hired again. By anyone. For anything.

She had a lot of explaining to do; beginning with the reason she didn't do the shoot in the morning when she played a page. That Mr. Lucas was in error would not clear her. Nobody had given her any kind of guidance, and she knew better than to use the "stocky red-faced Irishman" who happened to be *Mr. Griffith's assistant* as the reason for the foul-up.

What she learned next was quite a surprise. Nobody had told her. Not even the people at the front foyer window.

The Biograph Company was going to California!

California was far away from the Edison Company, who were trying to make competing film studios purchase Edison film stock for their productions. In the wake of the sudden proliferation of societies that were uniting Christians for the Suppression of Vice, California was the light at the end of the tunnel.

It was time to Go West. It was time to follow the Sun.

They'll never chase us this far seemed to be the attitude of Biograph and several studios who saw the Edison vigilantes as little better than organized thugs who wanted nothing more than to bully the "washboard and sink" studios and Jersey City into submission and surrender.

Griffith, who was on friendly terms with Edison and purchased Edison film stock, saw the Edison unannounced raids as the first steps to convince Biograph to merge. To join with Edison was something he violently opposed. Their views on filmmaking were quite different. Edison saw motion pictures as a tool for education, while Griffith saw films as an entertainment industry.

California was an opportunity to make authentic Westerns in a real Western setting, rather than use the mountains of Coytesville or Plainfield, New Jersey.

As Griffith envisioned this great transference, there would be a company of twenty-seven people, including Mack, Linda (Mrs. Griffith) Arvidson, and the three Pickfords (Mary, her brother Jack, acting as his sister's chaperon at Mrs. Pickford's insistence and Mrs. Pickford herself).

Noticeably absent for this seven-month venture which would begin in January 1910, was Mabel Normand.

Mack knew it was time to allow his mentor exercise full control. Griffith didn't want Mabel around in any capacity—actress, wardrobe person, or travel companion.

Mack just had to be there, and to be available, even if it meant only being at Mr. Griffith's side, or to walk with him from the hotel to the location where the shoot would take place. It would be like the old days when he was little more than a "gopher."

Mabel would be left behind to fend for herself. There wouldn't be anyone to guide her. Being able to protect one's self was something she had learned how to do.

Mack never made any real commitment to her, and he knew better than to hint that there was a girl he would sometimes bring to the Metropolitan Opera House and take to the cheap seats. Did his mother want a girl for him?

Mabel's mother, he knew, would oppose her choice of beau. *Any* beau.

Exactly what was he? How would Mabel describe him to gain favor? A "stocky red-faced Irishman" who still spat tobacco juice on the floor whenever he felt he wanted to? That description would never change.

The nature of their friendship was a secret, even to themselves...

Chapter 6
Chances

Since the earliest days of filmmaking, truth and lore were often inextricable. Insiders knew there were two kinds of the *actual* truth. 1) What actually was witnessed and could be verified, and 2) what the studios told their players to say in newspaper and fan magazines, via press agents. So long as the mix sold copies for the benefit of the studios and the players, all was well and there were no problems.

A player to whom audiences responded in a positive manner and had money-making potential was given an identity and an off-screen persona. Mary Pickford and her golden curls was Our Mary. Mabel Normand and her hoydenish ways was Madcap Mabel.

That Mabel wasn't going to be part of the group going to California, while Mack was, concerned Griffith's relationship with Mack and its future possibilities. Mack was still a good person in whom Griffith could confide his ideas and ask for opinions. Ostensibly attempting to keep his relations with Mack on a solid base, Griffith suggested to Mabel that she take the subway to the Flatbush section of Brooklyn and offer her service to Vitagraph. The travel distance was longer, but Vitagraph paid a slightly better salary if the applicant had had some before-the-camera experience, and showed some potential. While the extra salary was certainly needed to support her family, Mabel was also aware she would never escape the hovering insecurity that co-existed in an uneasy alliance with each prospect of employment. *How long will this job last?* At the end of each shoot, the player realized he or she would be starting anew at square one. *If they wanted you back...*

Mabel knew her association with Mack did not deliver any emotional commitment other than being a *pal*, something adolescents were. Other young girls her age were thinking of getting married just to get away from their families. That she was aware that these marriages often put a young girl under more pressure than she ever experienced meant nothing. Mack, at the age of twenty-eight, was a *man* old enough to accept responsibility.

Neither Mack nor Mabel ever formalized their relationship or thought of any future date for a wedding. They might have shared a few kisses at night on the Staten Island Ferry, but there never was a *Will you marry me?* proposal, or an indication that she should be expecting one. Both Mack and Mabel had mothers, and neither could predict their reactions.

Blanche Sweet, casually observing the two of them on the Biograph lot, told the writer:

> "The two of them were like young school children just before adolescence. They weren't secure with themselves. The two of them were silly kids trying to sneak away from their mothers just to steal a kiss, like the song says, 'In the Shade of the Old Apple Tree.' Mabel was like a tomboy, always joking with the crew, acting like she was their *pal* instead of a woman, even though she was only sixteen years old.
>
> "I guess it was easier for her that way. She carried his ring, and she would sometimes wear it, but it gave the impression that neither Mack nor Mabel was aware of the implications. Mack was still finding humor spitting tobacco in any direction he chose, and we never saw Mabel trying to tell him privately or publicly to improve his manners.
>
> "Maybe she thought if she criticized him, he

would never ask her to marry him. Maybe he would leave her. And then what to do. Her career wasn't going in any direction at this point.

"In front of people, Mabel was a lot of fun, but men don't marry tomboys, and when Mack left Mabel to go to California with Mr. Griffith, she was on her own…"

Vitagraph was Biograph's biggest competitor, turning out a reel a week since its first program at Tony Pastor's New Fourteenth Street Theatre on March 23, 1896. Vitagraph, in addition to its stable of performers drawn from stock companies, vaudeville, and unknowns who took the chance and went there by subway to make their presence known to the front window personnel, had attained some significance by wisely filming the funeral cortege accompanying the casket of the recently assassinated President William McKinley.

Mabel's initial weeks at Vitagraph were not unlike those of any new employee. She had to find her way on her own without any help.

Until she met John Bunny.

Brooklyn-born Bunny was a heavy character player, whose career went from minstrel shows to roles in touring Shakespeare plays, particularly as Sir Toby Belch, Friar Laurence, and Falstaff. The publicity makers released the story that John Bunny was seen in the Vitagraph yard by executives J. Stuart Blackton and Albert E. Smith. Unlike the other hopefuls who might have been handsome or beautiful, Bunny realized that his onstage visual appeal could possibly transfer to onscreen appeal.

The camera loved faces, and his large face and endearing smile would be a perfect foil to Mabel who would later be a wonderful foil to Roscoe Arbuckle.

The career of John Bunny lasted from 1910 to his premature death at the age of fifty-one in 1915, after an unsuccessful English tour of an original musical comedy he backed with his own money, *Bunny in Funnyland*.

Some critics found Mabel's character a "little too free with her hugging and kissing," in *The Troublesome Secretaries* opposite John Bunny, with whom she got along both professionally and privately. She, Bunny, and the very thin Flora Finch were a perfect screen comedy trio: heavy John Bunny, a voluptuous Mabel and her dark mysterious eyes, and visually comic Flora, just barely fitting in on the right side of the screen. The audience loved the visual contrasts their sizes afforded, but some critics believed Mabel's acting was lacking in taste and refinement.

Under contract to Vitagraph at the same time were three Brooklyn-born sisters whose anxiety-ridden mother's home was an Ocean Avenue, a few streets away from the studio. Norma Talmadge, the youngest of the three, was brought to the front office by Peg Talmadge, who always told prospective employers to kindly address her as *Mother* Talmadge, to give the impression that she was a lady and a *Mother* worthy of *respect*, as were her *highly supervised* daughters.

Norma (born in 1903) had a good deal of experience, beginning her career as a youngest posing for illustrated slides shown on the screen with song lyrics for the audience to sing-a-long as the projectionist changed reels.

Natalie (born 1901) and the oldest, Constance (born 1899), went directly into *films* just before the Gish sisters (Lillian and Dorothy) were signed at Biograph (1912).

Concerned that Mabel's antics and unchaperoned late-night revels might lead her into situations that would be beyond her control, Peg Talmadge, seeing the friendship developing between her daughter Norma and Mabel, decided it was time to be a mentor to the very impressionable Mabel. If one could watch over three, one more would not be that difficult, she thought…

Constance recalled the situation to the author at the Booth Theatre in New York in May 1968.

> "Both Mabel and my sister Norma hit it off almost from the moment they met at Vitagraph. Mabel was a little wild and untamed for a female, which is why she was called 'Madcap Mabel.' She was beautiful,

and she was fearless. She did her own stunts and she was a good diver and swimmer. Had she started her career two or three years later, *she* would have had Pearl White's career. But Pearl's career didn't last as long as Mabel's, and Mabel did quite a lot of harm to herself...

"We all partied and we all liked good times, but my mother raised us to listen to her, and to *look* and *learn*. We would look for a rich man, and try to learn if he was worth anything.

"My mother brought us into this business of moviemaking because we were living almost a month-to-month existence. We had no father, and we knew if we stuck together and helped our mother survive by keeping her around us and watching us, we'd make out all right. My mother, as well as the three of us, was fascinated by Mabel. We never knew if what she said about herself was totally true. She told a Hearst reporter [Adela Rogers St. John, her greatest advocate] that she was an orphan, that she had consumption and almost died before she was eight years old, that she worked long hours in a garment factory that was just like the Triangle Shirtwaist Factory.

"So she knew how to take care of herself. But she never knew what to do about Mack, who was the worst thing that could have happened to her, or any girl. His movies were funny, and they made us laugh, but life is not like the movies. Away from the studio world, he was a vulgar man who never offered Mabel any future or any indication of security. She just lived for today, and she never thought there would be a tomorrow.

"My mother taught us how to save and invest our money. She told Mabel to do the same thing. When we met Mabel on the Vitagraph set in Brooklyn, Mack was in California. I don't know if they were keeping in touch. She was Norma's pal, not mine nor Natalie's.

"My mother constantly told Mabel to stay away from Mack, that he was just taking up her time and not making any kind of promise. All of us were friendly and polite to Mabel, but we stopped advising her. Some people in this business know how to fend for themselves, some don't. My sisters and I listened. Mabel was just…Mabel."

In California, to Sennett's surprise, Griffith asked Frank Powell, one of his assistants, to direct *Comrades*. Powell, a cameraman, didn't feel he was quite able to do the direction. Griffith then asked Del Henderson, a pal of Sennett's, to direct the film and to co-star with Mack, a fellow Canadian with whom there was a natural off-screen chemistry that might be easily transferred.

Frank Capra, initially a screenwriter for Sennett before he became a director, explained Sennett's sudden, on-the-set logic before he and the author were going to tape a *Joe Franklin* television show on New York's WOR-TV, Channel 9.

"I wasn't present for the filming of *Comrades*, Stuart, but I could imagine how Sennett was in those days [1911]. As chaotic as those films may look, he wanted a smooth shoot, with everything pre-planned to *look* as spontaneous as possible.

"Any director wants his first effort to turn out well, or on schedule, and without any unexpected mishaps. It is why you surround yourself with people on whom you can depend."

Still regarded as one of Griffith's stable of actors despite a nice reception given to *Comrades*, Sennett went in front of the camera to play opposite Vivian Prescott in the role of a suspicious barber in *The Manicure Lady* who resents the attentions she pays to the constant stream of customers. Earlier, in *The Italian Barber*, Sennett was a very jealous Monsieur Dupont in the Griffith-directed version.

The group returned to Biograph in New York with mixed feelings at the end of July. Griffith, realizing the value, cinematically, of the natural scenery, had seen the advantage to film stories with Western themes, Spanish themes, and Indian themes. A California oil field was perfect for *The Gold Seekers*. The Border States was ideal for a Civil War drama.

While Sennett knew that none of Griffith's themes would ever excite his curiosity to the degree of wanting to explore them as future material, he took advantage of always being on the set to ask questions about Griffith's newest techniques in cross-cutting to show parallel action. Every day spent with Griffith was to learn a lesson from the master.

Griffith, he was told, was also thinking of expanding the length of his productions. Wouldn't it be possible to shoot two films at the same time, if one was the continuation of the other? Magazine stories were often continued and concluded in the next issue. Why not motion pictures? Why not release them to theatres as a *single* feature, and double the running time of the current one-reelers?

Frank Powell could handle the comedies, and Sennett would be given more directorial responsibilities as Griffith's *official* assistant.

One month after the Sennett-Griffith troupe had started to head

East for Biography, Mabel's work for Vitagraph in Brooklyn was coming to an end. After her last three films (*A Dead Man's Honor, Piccola,* and *The Changing of Silas Marner*), she did not see much of a future opposite an ailing John Bunny.

Constance Talmadge explained Bunny's problem:

> "Norma, Mabel and John Bunny were friends with each other, but they never appeared together. It was lunchroom friendship with John Bunny. Sometimes the three of them ate together and just talked, and laughed.
>
> "John was playing all kinds of characters—sea-captains, a lonely old man whose only companion was his dog…John was a wonderful dialect comedian. He was a master of accents, and the only way he could use these accents was on the stage. He would take a few months away from Vitagraph and go to England and do Shakespeare plays.
>
> "A lot of stage actors liked being in the films, *but it was strictly for the money.* Nothing else. I know he was sensitive about his weight, and the more popular he became, the more he thought he could *extend* his popularity if he would lose a few pounds. Mabel told him he was crazy. You don't ruin what you worked so long to develop. But the camera, he would say, is making him look like a balloon.
>
> "So when John returned, we noticed how much weight he had lost. Mabel privately told me John didn't look good, but she said nothing.

> "Comedy depends on contrast. One person is fat, the other is thin. One is tall, the other short. Mabel was just starting to make a name for herself. What would she do if her partner died? Could she get work without him? Who would be her foil? Please remember—neither Mack nor Mabel had done any films together. Everything was a *dream*, especially the question she wanted Mack to ask when he returned from California.

> "She would talk about it sometimes, but we didn't know what to say to her. Everything was up to him. The man asks the question. The lady accepts or rejects it."

In his autobiography, *King of Comedy*, Mack states Mabel's reaction when he was thinking of first declaring his *possible* intentions:

> "I dunno know about you, Mack Sennett. I don't know whether you are a man to fall in love with or not."

Sennett confesses to the reader:

> "The girl is romantic...and I am acting like a clown. I have got to write something romantical."

But he never did. His *own* words were never there.
And they *both* knew it...
Summertime and making motion pictures in New York were never compatible. The Caudebec Inn in the Orange Mountains of New York State was the ideal location to be utilized for the latest Griffith project, *The Diving Girl*, a half-reeler featuring Mabel Normand.

Mabel had been hired in deference to Sennett's constant entreaties. Griffith wasn't very fond of Mabel, as Blanche Sweet told the author.

> "To Mr. Griffith, moviemaking was a serious business, like an art form. He didn't really have a sense of humor, and he honestly believed that comedy on the screen was for peasants and uneducated people. He would have liked his audiences to view his films the same way they would dress to go to the theatre or the opera.
>
> "I think he was in conflict with his inner feelings, a *man's* feelings. You could look at a pretty girl, but don't let them catch you. He liked pretty blonde girls like Mary [Pickford] and me. We were innocent types the way Lillian and Dorothy Gish were.
>
> "*Looking* innocent meant you were pure, which transferred very well to the screen. If you had dark hair, dark eyes, or were Spanish, you were mysterious. Latins and Mediterraneans meant shifty, sneaky, lusty, and they were always a threat.
>
> "He refused to employ Valentino as the style of leading man had started to change in the 1920s and ladies began to have screen fantasies of their own."

In an effort to maintain the anonymity of his players, Griffith, at first, did not give them screen billing when audiences wanted to know the identities of the people they were frequently seeing on the screen with increasing rapidity.

It was an attitude used by many directors of the day, recalled Beverly Hills realtor, Jack Hupp, whose father, Earle Rodney, was a

Sennett player in the silent era, and later a screenwriter for Sennett contract player, Bing Crosby:

> "There was a kind of fame-and-shame attitude in those very early days. The money brought you fame, but it was rough for actors to purchase decent homes. There was a 'no dogs, no actors' philosophy that was quite open.
>
> "Many producers would never give any publicity because of the idea that the actor might ask for more money. So he was kept on as low a salary as possible. In England, they went so far as to change the name of the actor and give him another name! Mack Sennett was named Walter Terry. Mabel Normand was called Muriel Fortesque. Mary Pickford was always Mary Pickford from the moment she made her screen debut. She knew how to get her dollars and she knew when to ask for more dollars."

The snows of winter reminded Griffith of the advantages of filming in California—natural scenery, longer days, and the lack of an Edison raid by his goon squad who wanted only Edison stock, not Kodak, to be utilized in the filming process. When Mabel returned to Biograph, her first film, *The Diving Girl*, featured her in a bathing suit more suited to Griffith's highly-developed self-imposed propriety.

While Mack would not openly argue his theories on female presences on the screen, he knew that as the twentieth century progressed, fads and tastes of men would slowly adjust and adapt to an increasingly freer society.

Griffith's persistent casting of Mabel in melodramas was a perfect example of casting against type. Even with a rose in her hair, she would not have seemed to make a better Carmen-type vamp. Men sensed it was all a game and not to be taken seriously.

Blanche Sweet stated it to the author quite succinctly:

> "Just walking into a room from another room, you laughed, just seeing her. She waited for Mack, and waited, and waited. Inside, she must have been very sad…"

Mabel was part of the company when Griffith made his second trip to California. Blanche was also part of the troupe, which also included newcomer Donald Crisp, a former writer for *The Smart Set* magazine. Crisp, like Lillian Gish, with whom he would later work, was one of the applicants hired at the 14th Street window. What he may have lacked in dramatic experience was temporarily put aside because of his overpowering presence.

The new outdoor studio had significant improvements from the first, Blanche Sweet told this writer, based on Mary Pickford's recollections.

> "Mary told me the first studio was on Grand Avenue and Washington Streets on what was nothing more than a vacant lot. We had very little furniture, and if we didn't have too much wind, the flats wouldn't blow in the breeze. We had to change in the nearby hotel and make our way over.
>
> "The new place was in a different area [Georgia and Girard Streets]. The stage was smoother and there were *real* dressing rooms and running water, and a *telephone!*"

At the beach in Santa Monica, Mabel and her direct opposite, Mary Pickford, were cast in *The Mender of Nets*. With a script written by Edwin August, this Griffith two-reeler was an indication of the detail Griffith was to show in his future work—Mary's long golden curls, and Mabel's dark hair. Mary's purity and Mabel's almost vampish presence set against the background of the sea.

Blanche Sweet, who was not in the film, recalled:

> "Griffith was constantly paying strict attention to the backgrounds of his films. His establishing shots always let the audience know where the story was going to take place, the way an author does. Remember, Mr. Griffith was a *playwright* first, and he always said he was going to return to the theatre. Luckily for motion pictures and us, he never did. We spent quite a lot of time together, Mabel, Mary and myself.
>
> "Men were a little afraid of Mary. She watched everything. She took everything in. Mabel was a fun, goodtime girl. On the train, she taught me how to smoke a cigarette, and we had to do this in secret, because only low-class girls smoked. Whenever they wanted to show a girl with bad morals, they showed her with a cigarette in her mouth, and the cigarette always hung from her lower lip.
>
> "Both Mary and Mabel were voracious readers, but for different reasons. Mabel read to educate herself, and Mary was always looking for stories which could be used as vehicles for her films.
>
> "Both Mary and Mr. Griffith were are of copyrights and not trying to *lift* anything from an already well-known work. A piece of literature written by someone who is still living.
>
> "Mary also had other problems—behind her mother's back, before we came to California,

> Mary had gone to Jersey City, New Jersey dressed in her mother's clothes, to look older (she was only 17) to marry Owen Moore, an actor she met at Biograph. He was much older and her mother had *never* liked him.
>
> "If Mabel ever said anything about it, she didn't talk about it to me. Everyone did things without everyone knowing about it. Mack was still spending time after the shooting day had ended with Mr. Griffith. Mabel and I used to go to the Pier or Levy's café. We used to laugh when we would hear that people wanted to be in pictures. Sometimes *we* used to wish *we* could be like everybody else and have a life of our own."

The Mender of Nets was Griffith's biggest success. His direction and Mary's performance were perfection. And they knew it.

Mary left Biograph to work for IMP (Independent Motion Picture Company) at a larger salary—$175 a week. With her mother, brother Jack, and sister Lottie they moved into a respectable bungalow.

Owen, who had been independent until now, was soon overwhelmed by the number of people in his *wife's* family living together in such cramped (for him) quarters. When he started drinking out of his inability to be accepted as his *own* man, and *not* only as the husband of Mary Pickford, the marriage had started to fall apart within the year.

Blanche Sweet observed:

> "Mary was heartbroken over the mistake she had made in marrying Owen Moore. *Suddenly* she was aware that he was a much older and experienced *man*, while she was, with her long golden curls, *a very little girl*. And all of this proved to Mary that her

mother Charlotte, who opposed the marriage from the beginning, was *absolutely right*. And that Mary had better do something fast. Things would have to be changed."

At the studio Mack received a letter from his mother which praised the progress he was making. She also noted that his meager salary (not for the times, but compared to huge amounts of money the studio was making) of $75 a week was far below what she thought he was worth.

Perhaps it was necessary for her to take the train to California to talk to him, and the studio heads as well. Something was *wrong*.

Mack may have been within a few years of forty, but he was still her baby boy. And would always be regarded as that.

Some things could *not* be changed...

Chapter 7
Golden Gates

"I know the younger generations speak of Mack and Mabel as one of the great Hollywood love stories that, over the decades, has assumed almost epic proportions. *Not to those of us at Biograph, who were witnesses at the time*..."

—Blanche Sweet
Conversation with the author, May 1976

1912. From his mentor Griffith, Mack was still learning how to act in front of a camera, and how to structure and make a film. He was absorbing everything, including how to act. Even though the presence of Mabel was something fellow Biograph players were accustomed to seeing, Mack knew when it was the right time to allow Mr. Griffith to assume priority.

Both gentlemen, while courteous to each other, still greatly differed on the type of motion picture they wanted to make, and the type of audience that would attend them. Griffith was partial to the action film and the comedies of manners that were very popular in the theatre. It was in these comedies of manners that he started as a touring stock company actor, and had tried to write as a young playwright.

Mack, lacking Griffith's theatrical experience, wanted to use his burlesque and vaudeville experience that he believed would transfer to the screen quite easily. A pretty girl and physical humor. He believed that he had found both elements in Mabel. *The Diving*

Girl, filmed at Coney Island prior to going to California, Sennett thought was the perfect showcase.

But Griffith still wouldn't yield. Mabel was a *comedienne*, a voluptuous woman, a far cry from the virginal Blanche Sweet, Mary Pickford and Mae Marsh type that had been popular with the audiences who frequented the nickelodeons on 14th Street.

Griffith's women were synonymous with purity and respect, a type that Lillian and Dorothy Gish, who were soon to be hired within the year, would come to personify.

From the moment Mabel, in her form-fitting bathing suit, gave the cameraman a very desirable profile before diving off the pier at Coney Island, Sennett knew this was just what the male audiences wanted to see. Over and over again.

Donald Crisp, a recently hired player, summed up Mabel's appeal quite succinctly. "Every man loved Mabel…given the chance."

If Mack ever gave any indication that he was aware of Mabel's or any other player's away-from-the-camera romances or relationships, he gave no indication. Just before Mack, Mabel, Blanche and cameraman Billy Bitzer were preparing to go to California, Mack received a surprise visit…from his mother.

Amongst the players at any studio, or the actors at any theatre, there were never any secrets. Everyone became a family, a family that would protect each other from the newspapers and the *outside* world. Inside the gates was *another* world, a world of security and shelter.

Catherine Sinnott's sudden visit was a signal to band together in a spirit of protection against disapproval from an outside force of disapproval, be it civilians or family members.

Catherine Sinnott wasn't a stage mother who wanted the best for her son. She was the *other* mother—a disapproving type who wanted her son to fail. It would provide the perfect *I told you so*, and follow this with rantings about *bad people* and *loose women*, good reasons to make Mack leave.

Unknown to her, Mack and Mabel had become secretly engaged on a nighttime ferry boat that made crossings to Staten Island. The ring had cost two dollars, and it was probably Mack's *second* attempt at independence from his family.

The first attempt was his leaving Canada to enter the uncertain world of the opera and the theatre. Both attempts to succeed had failed. It was only in the *vulgar* world of burlesque in the Bowery, and in the few touring companies, that he would be able to earn some money to pay for his rented room to be held in New York when he returned. The price could go up in his absence.

Mabel, sensing problems, removed the engagement ring and placed it at the bottom of her purse, where it would remain.

To fellow Biograph employees who asked why Mack hadn't asked *The Question*, Mabel would answer in a soft voice, "Mack hasn't asked me."

And then there was a polite silence. It was understood.

According to Blanche Sweet, in whom Mabel confided, the meeting between Mrs. Sinnott and Mabel was cordial. Mack's mother was happy to see that her bachelor son had finally found *someone* with whom he could settle down.

But Mack knew how his mother *really* felt. Mabel, Madcap Mabel, was a wildly impulsive person who might not want to really settle down, leaving the business of picture-making, and become a mother capable of raising proper children. Whenever Mrs. Sinnott was *too* pleased, there had to be a hidden, opposite reason. *Too* pleased meant very unhappy. *Too* much encouragement, Mack knew, was her way of being displeased.

Mabel would tell her co-workers at Biograph that she was *waiting* and Mack would still be absorbed in his career and loaded with new projects.

In his autobiography he would confess, "I just couldn't do it."

Both Mack and Mabel were insecure, and had doubts about each other.

Blanche remarked:

> "I was raised by my grandmother, who put me on the stage to earn a living for us. I always had her approval.
>
> "Mack broke away from his home and the *more* success he had, the more he wanted approval from his mother. It just wasn't

there. It never was there, and she sent him money in the early days so he wouldn't have to come home to his small Canadian village and *admit* she was right.

"That would be the unkindest cut of all—to admit your disapproving family was right. That they were always right, and you had to come home to the small town. It is as if they *wanted* you to fail.

"I don't know if Mack would actually tell his mother that he and Mabel were engaged. She rarely wore the ring, and she never returned it after their fights."

Mack knew not to always have Mabel at his side when he was talking about the craft of filmmaking. Griffith's marriage to Linda Arvidson was in trouble and Mack knew not to ask his mentor if he should tie the knot with Mabel. One of the lessons he had learned from Griffith was that being creative was a full-time job to which one devoted one's life. Wives, children, and families, while *sometimes* supportive and encouraging, never completely understood what went on inside an artist's mind.

Griffith's seeming logic provided Mack with an appropriate answer to questions about how much longer would the engagement last: "I don't know. It's up to her."

And in Mack's own mind—"Perhaps in California."

Perhaps the sunshine and the beaches would change her mind. California was a place where a lot of people would go to start their lives again.

Chapter 8
From Dreams to Decisions

The galloping tintypes and "flickers" that once condescendingly described and dismissed the nickelodeon nickel-and-dime 14th Street was patronized by those with limited education, illiterates, and recently arrived immigrants—people who were happy just to duck in for a few minutes of escapism.

Legitimate theatre actors, realizing there was a good dollar to be made on their day off, began to inquire about the suitability of utilizing their talents with the idea of reaching a larger audience when they would return to the stage. That Laurette Taylor, Maude Adams, and the Barrymores (John, Ethel and Lionel) would temporarily sweep aside their integrity and take a "flier" into cinema, without the sound of their voices, was understood by fellow professionals. Artists, too, needed to eat.

But the class system would still secretly exist amongst the purists on both sides of the footlights.

Wise film producers often lure theatre actors with promises of acting under a *different* name, should they even have dreams of returning to the discipline of eight shows a week with a Wednesday and Saturday matinee. And then touring.

Often popularity in a stage vehicle made an actor unable to consider any other opportunity but to remain with the play. Shakespearean actor James (father of playwright Eugene) O'Neill was so successful as *The Count of Monte Cristo* that he toured with the play for *forty* years. The role of Edmond Dantes was such a *tour de force* that the good salary made him *forced to tour!* And he *filmed* the play. And toured *again*.

Sarah Bernhardt's *Queen Elizabeth*, playing at New York's Lyceum Theatre, was considered her bid for immortality when the play was *filmed*.

Indeed, studios began to proliferate in New York and the surrounding areas—Thanhouser (New Rochelle), Bigelow (Stamford, Connecticut), Dandy Films, Essanay (Chicago), and in New Jersey—Edison (West Orange), Solax (Fort Lee), Nestor (Bayonne), and Pathé Freres (Jersey City and Bound Brook).

All of these emerging decisions to develop the bourgeoning industry did not bypass Sennett or Griffith. Griffith had visions of two- and three-reelers and even features, and Mack wanted to return to California, the perfect setting for comedies with beach settings and bathing beauties.

The beaches were free. With the girls you could negotiate.

What would be funnier than bathing beauties chasing policemen or vice-versa?

Laughing at figures of authority—what could be funnier? It was the subject over which Sennett and Griffith often disagreed.

On his own, without the needed approval of his mentor, Sennett could make all of the decisions. He would develop his *own* ensemble.

But what would he call his new place?

As motion picture folklore would have it, and anyone in the film business can tell you—good press agentry and time equal truth. Sennett, during the course of a lunch meeting at Delmonico's in New York with two bookies (Charles Bauman and Adam Kessel) to whom he owed an unpaid racetrack debt from excursions to Belmont Park, put forth a proposal neither man would refuse: invest $2,500 of their own money, removing the $100 debt Sennett owed, and invest in Sennett's new motion-picture company in California.

California?

Like a fast-talking press agent, Sennett continued.

Sunshine, pretty girls, beautiful beaches.

No more fears of Edison's goon-squad detectives forcing the purchase of Edison film stock.

And California is across the country. In California you can leave your past behind you, and start all over again.

CHAPTER 8: FROM DREAMS TO DECISIONS | 167

And here is when fiction and fact are inextricably mixed.

When the three men left Delmonico's and started walking, a train from Pennsylvania Station sounded in their vicinity. On one of the railroad cars: *Keystone*.

The new studio had its name, and they didn't have to pay for copyrights.

Prior to the trip west, there were problems to be cleared up at Biograph…

Blanche Sweet told the writer what she had started to notice.

> "The ongoing relationship of Mack and Mabel was a continuing good-day, bad-day, on and off, off and on thing. I think the two of them, after being together for so long, were wary of each other. *He* was never forthright about his intentions, and I think she was afraid she was going to play second fiddle to his mother. They were two scared children who were too old to be children. Maybe she should have told him she was pregnant, but that means you have to make *assumptions*…And that was something you never talked about except in whispers and to people you can trust to keep a secret."

Mack's final days at Biograph, prior to his departure for California, were filled with personal commitments that needed to be honored regarding Mabel and two-reelers with Mabel that had to be completed.

Behind his back, the female players at Biograph were calling him a "lout," for stringing Mabel along and not giving any indication that one day their "association" would be "legal."

As the days drew closer to the departure date, Mack's mother paid an unexpected visit.

Blanche Sweet recalled:

> "It was as if she *instinctively* knew when to crash the party, and throw all of the secret

preparations askew. Depending on whose side you are taking, perfect timing became the *wrong* moment, or the *right* moment to further damage his and Mabel's life.

"Because Mack was still beholden to Mr. Griffith, he never asked for a raise. Mack knew that Mr. Griffith's films were prestigious, but he also knew that a Mabel Normand one- or two-reeler always rounded out the program *and* was always a crowd-pleaser. Mabel, at that time, was always the good source of box office returns.

"With his mother, I was told, Mack went to Mr. Griffith's office and after some haggling, was given a raise to sustain him until he would leave for California. Both men fully knew what had happened— Mack, under Mr. Griffith's tutelage, had gone about as far as he could go.

"Both men also knew that Mr. Griffith was not fond of Mabel, and Mabel knew that one day Mack might be asked to make a decision regarding her future. She knew she had no chance of a future if Mack left, and she was left behind.

"Even before Mack approached Mabel with an idea for slapstick policemen, Mary's attitude was similar to Mr. Griffith's—the law was to be respected, and she would not allow her golden curls, which were her trademark, to be associated with any form of roughhouse or knockabout.

"Mary had already broken with Biograph,
and it was time for Mack to follow suit."

With their increasing popularity, Mack and Mabel had found their voices. What had to be further developed could only be done in California.

Chapter 9
The Ending and the Beginning

While Griffith and Sennett remained openly professional and cordial on the Biography lot, it was an open secret that both men wanted to leave New York. Griffith, seeing a future in features, wanted to build a larger studio on 175th Street in the Bronx, while Sennett, who saw no future in New York, was now considering the area in 1912 with greater possibilities.

Frankly tired of the "moralistic Griffith melodramas" on which he learned his craft, he saw his future in comedies, which Griffith, who still wished to eventually abandon motion pictures once he made *enough* money, viewed as vulgar entertainment for immigrants. He belonged in the theatre.

Once a theatre man, always a theatre man. Griffith's roots, he would constantly remind Sennett, were in playwriting and acting on the stage. Sennett's were in cheap vaudeville and burlesque.

Sennett's wishes were well known as he completed his final days on East 14th Street station.

At the end of August 1912, Sennett, with his loyal company of Fred Mace, Ford Sterling, and Mabel Normand, boarded the train at Grand Central Station for Los Angeles. Unlike Griffith, whose goals were always artistic, Sennett's were totally mercenary. He wanted to make *money*, and he wanted to do it with Griffith-like discipline—a film a week would please the greatest number of people possible. That his audience may have been barely literate immigrants made no difference. The test of ultimate success was still the box office.

One thing was for certain—Mary Pickford wanted no part of his California venture. Her opposition to his ideas of using policemen as figures of ridicule would always remain constant.

Mr. Sennett's theories weren't humorous. They were vulgar. Just as he was.

After a five-day, four-night cross-country trip, the train carrying Mack, Mabel, and the others arrived at the Santa Fe station in Los Angeles on September 12.

While the eager foursome saw Los Angeles as the beginning of a wonderful future, many older citizens, who were long accustomed to a population of 30,000 and rich areas of orange groves, did not welcome the influx of wandering players standing at the gates. Several realtors, bowing to growing resentment regarding the newly developing film industry had placed "No dogs, No Jews, No Actors" adjacent to "For Sale" signs on available properties as a deterrent to anyone who had plans to settle in wealthier areas.

This less than subtle admonition meant nothing to the four travelers, who had long been accustomed to various kinds of harassment, having performed and lived in all kinds of conditions. The off-stage life of any actor was not without its risks and prejudices heaped upon them from the same people, who just applauded them when the curtain came down.

The risk taker was Mabel, who, without much of a bank account and no real stage or vaudeville experience, had made the cross-country trip on Black Diamond Express from Jersey City, New Jersey, changed at Chicago's La Salle Street station for the California Limited to the Santa Fe Station in Los Angeles.

Mabel wasn't chasing after a career in movies. She was willing to chase after Mack, no matter where he went. Even to Los Angeles.

Like his mentor, D.W. Griffith, a woman like Mabel was strictly *talent*, disposable, or non-disposable. Mabel, he knew, was a great talent. She could do anything, but get Mack to propose to her, and she was willing to live anywhere.

Mack, having lived in rooming houses and cheap hotels since he first entered show business, was not looking for a home, certainly not a home in an area that was so open about its feelings toward the arts, and the participants.

A *home* in any area was synonymous with permanence, marriage, and *Mama*. Mama and marriage were certainly the last things on his mind. The less baggage, humor or otherwise, would make it easier for him to survive in a profession of constant uncertainty.

A hotel was most desirable. He judged the hotels by their accessibility to the studio, the price and quality of the available room, whether the management would be tolerant of actors, and whether their occasional minor weaknesses and lapses in proper morality could be tolerated. Occasional "guest" or no, the word "double" on the hotel register served as a protection, as long as the visitor *wasn't* a minor.

The ever-thirty Sennett hoped that the management would be willing to look the other way, should Mabel decide to stay the night. Mama, should she pay a surprise visit, could always stay in a vacant room, but Mabel had to be off the premises.

Remembering that the New York Athletic Club provided a room when the gymnasium was to be used for an overnight stay, he looked for a similar arrangement with the Los Angeles Athletic Club.

Mabel, for the first few days, had a room at the more elegant Hotel Alexandria, the scene of many end-of-the-day's parties, and completion-of-the-film parties. Most of the actors always attended, but to Mabel's amazement, few actually *lived* on the premises.

According to the surviving contemporaries in 1968, Mabel's addresses, depending on her finances, were in a constant state of flux—the Baltic apartments in the Echo Park area, a "white stucco building" where Bates and Fountain Avenue met, Seventh and Figueroa…

When Blanche Sweet came to Los Angeles the following year (1913), Mabel lived at Blanche's grandmother's home on Manzanita Street until she could get herself together.

Blanche Sweet remembered Mabel's longer-than-anticipated stay.

> "Mr. Griffith took his Biography troupe to California to film *Judith of Bethulia*. I was Judith, the leading role, and this was Mr. Griffith's first attempt at making something longer than two reels. [It was four reels.]
>
> "I was only seventeen, and this feature cost

Chapter 9: The Ending and the Beginning

Mack Sennett, Mabel Normand & Ford Sterling.

$50,000! Had Sennett stayed with Mr. Griffith, he could have been part of the action, but I think this film was a test for both men. Mr. Griffith knew he had to grow up, and Sennett had to grow, period. Comedies were his only chance to create something original, to use all audiences. Not only immigrants.

"I think Mack's feelings toward Mabel remained unchanged. I would talk, and talk, and plead with Mabel, when she stayed with us, *not* to put up with Mack's shenanigans anymore. It was time to step up to the plate, and declare his intentions.

"I'd talk far into the night. Often, I had to be

drunk enough in order to say what I really thought. And she was drunk, too, and in the morning, neither of us could remember the conversation of the night before, but I knew I had gotten it out of my system, and I felt the better for saying it.

"*Mack*, I told her, *was a 40-year-old Mama's boy. Is that what you want? A big sissy?* He's not starving, and you know what? You're not going to remember a word I said! A man like Mack never has enough—unless part of it goes to Mama. And when she comes to visit, he'll do what he's done before—concoct some reason or excuse to have a fight, just for the excuse of getting you to walk away. Why don't you *really* walk away? Keep your relationship strictly professional the way Mary [Pickford] did with Mr. Griffith. Mr. Griffith would never dare to try to take advantage of her! You and Mack have no future together. You're not even *living* together! Why don't you wake up, and finally open your eyes, and see Mack for what he really is? Then you can see what is really important in his life!"

To build a studio, his own studio, up from the ground. That was his big desire—to prove he could do such a thing! That would be his crowning achievement *for now*.

Keystone Studios!

Mack Sennett's Keystone Studios!

The Fun Factory!

And it would certainly impress—his mother, himself, and Mabel!

The Keystone or what was called a *studio* was in considerable disarray when Sennett arrived. Mabel had her own dressing room, and adjacent to it was a building where the other females dressed. The dressing rooms of the men were on the other side of the path that was the studio's entrance. The area before the studio gates consisted of junkyards, and tiny farms that were long ago abandoned.

The hot air was still, and everything was frozen in defiance of time.

But that would soon change. This was only the beginning.

Chapter 10
Trying to Match the Mentor

1914. With the arrival and acceptance of D.W. Griffith's biblical four-reeler, *Judith of Bethulia*, on March 8, the motion picture had begun to make its way out of the storefront nickelodeons and begin to make its presence known and accepted uptown at legitimate theatres.

In April, Griffith, with Lillian Gish as the leading lady, was on the motion picture screens with the *five*-reel, *The Battle of the Sexes*. In May, Lillian and Dorothy Gish were in the *six*-reeler, *Home Sweet Home*. In June, Griffith's *seven*-reeler, *The Escape*, was shown on New York theatre screens.

Using Edgar Allan Poe's *The Tell-Tale Heart* as source material, Griffith completed his August release, *The Avenging Conscience*, starring Blanche Sweet.

That Griffith was planning a twelve-reel film requiring weeks of shooting, utilizing thousands of men playing Union and Confederate soldiers, and have thousands of scenes before its completion was not lost on Mack Sennett or Mabel. Both Mack and Mabel did not know anything else, but they realized their efforts would be overshadowed so long as Mack was afraid to make a feature. Mabel did not want to be a one- or two-reeler actress whose work was confined to nickelodeons.

Blanche Sweet recalled Mabel's mounting insecurity as she saw rival studios starting to turn out products of greater lengths than Sennett's.

"Mabel would constantly keep asking Mack, 'When can I do a feature? When can I do a feature?' and Mack replied by giving her a fifty-thousand-dollar emerald engagement ring, which was very impressive to all of us, but when Mack walked away, she would drop the emerald ring into her purse, and take out the two-dollar engagement ring he gave her on the Staten Island Ferry when they both had nothing.

"There was more love and honesty in that earlier engagement ring. That other ring, she felt, meant more. This ring was a good show for Mack's mother. But we don't know what his mother thought of Mabel."

On Mack's mind was the recurring doubt—could Mabel carry a feature? Mack had never made a *feature*.

Charlie Chaplin's work, like Mabel's, was limited to one- and two-reelers. Could Chaplin's humor last long enough to carry a *feature*?

The rival Famous Players had successfully lured legitimate actors to the screen to repeat their stage triumphs—Sarah Bernhardt (*Queen Elizabeth*), James O'Neill (*The Count of Monte Cristo*), James K. Hackett (*The Prisoner of Zenda*).

All the aforementioned inspired Mack to attempt a full-length comedy. His choice—*Tillie's Nightmare*, a stage hit with Marie Dressler. Its screen title—*Tillie's Punctured Romance*. Would Miss Dressler appear in a Sennett film? Without sound, was she able to get the laughs? Was she able to sustain the attention of a *motion picture* audience?

After expressing his doubts concerning Marie's suitability, Mack's offer of $2,250 a week, with a guaranteed fourteen weeks, soothed her. The film would have a triple-treat cast to bring in the motion picture fans—Dressler, Charlie Chaplin, and Mabel Normand.

Tillie's Punctured Romance's cast would utilize the Sennett players *with one exception*.

Minta explained the one disagreement regarding the total casting to the author:

> "Everyone at Keystone was very excited except *Roscoe*. Dressler knew who Roscoe 'Fatty' Arbuckle was, and she had seen his work on screen, and she knew that he could play to the camera for maximum effect. Her reaction to Mack was two words: '*Not him*!' And then she pointed to herself. 'I am the star! I created this part in the theatre' as if we were less than nothing, only being *picture people*! As if 'picture' was a bad word, not deserving of any respect!
>
> "Mack tried to convince her that Roscoe's part wasn't as large as hers, but she wanted none of it. '*Two* fat people can't be in the same picture!'"

There was no room for argument. If Marie Dressler was going to be Mack's transition from one- and two-reelers and respect, he was going to go along with it.

The omission of Roscoe Arbuckle from the cast of twenty-three was an intentionally noticeable omission, which was mentioned more than once to Minta. When the question was put to her by the author, she nodded, as if in anticipation of when it would be asked.

She replied:

> "I'm glad that you asked. And let me tell you that Roscoe also asked the same question to Mack at the time the same way you are asking now [July 1968]. Mack's answer, according to Mack, was simple enough for him. Marie played the lead on Broadway, Marie is the reason we're making this film, and for the salary she's getting, I want her on the screen as often as I can get her up there. The public already knows Mabel and Charlie, and the public will come to see them in anything—even a supporting role.

I'm banking everything on Marie.

"Charlie and Mabel already have two pictures being released within a week of each other. [*His Musical Career*—one reel—November 7, 1914, and *His Trysting Place*—two reels—November 9, 1914.] That may have satisfied the public, but it never satisfied Roscoe, who had been very loyal to Mack ever since he was hired [May 1913] and made over 50 films!

"Mack certainly didn't fight for Roscoe the way Mabel fought for Charlie in his early days. I told Roscoe to forget about it, that *he'd* last longer. Marie didn't have his know-how.

"We spoke to Mabel, but she was so determined to get Mack to marry her, she'd do anything to keep her hopes up—especially since she was sporting that doorknob of a ring on that left hand whenever Mack was in the area."

Roscoe's judgment proved to be right. While Marie Dressler was hired to bring a certain respect to motion pictures, having created the role on stage, it was Chaplin who garnered the best box-office reviews.

True, Marie went to other studios afterwards, but she had to wait until the thirties and a *sound* comeback as Min, playing opposite Wallace Beery, in *Min and Bill* (1932). Until her "comeback" in the sound era, Marie Dressler would continue to be the heroine of the working-class woman, "the pride of Yokeltown, and the apple of her Papa's eye."

Tillie's Punctured Romance, the big gamble for Sennett, turned out to be a hit—for *Chaplin*.

From *Moving Picture World*:

> "Chaplin outdoes Chaplin—that's all there is to it. His marvelous right-footed skid—and it seems to make no difference whether he has under him rough highway or parlor floor—is just as funny in the last [6th] reel as it is in the first."

From *Variety*:

> "*Tillie's Punctured Romance* came from the title role Miss Dressler played in *Tillie's Nightmare*. She is splendidly supported by the Keystone Company, including Charles Chaplin, Mabel Normand, Mack Sennett, Mack Swain and others. Miss Dressler is the central figure, but Chaplin's camera antics are an essential feature in putting the picture over. Mack Sennett directed the picture and right well has he done his job."

With the completion of *Tillie's Punctured Romance*, the Chaplin-Normand-Arbuckle alliance begins to weaken.

Chaplin remained at Keystone, completing the one-reeler, *Getting Acquainted* (December 5, 1914), and the two-reeler, *His Prehistoric Past*, on December 7.

It was the on-the-paper end of Chaplin's employment at Keystone.

Minta recalled Chaplin's office meeting with Mack Sennett, which was to be his final one.

> "It was an open secret that Charlie would eventually leave. He had complete control over what he was doing. He was just getting under the wire, and Mack was always at him to beat the deadline. And Charlie always did! But he liked to have more time to tinker before he let it out for distribution.
>
> "Knowing that it was *he* and not Marie

Dressler who made *Tillie's Punctured Romance* a big success, especially with that tango dance he and Marie did, he wanted to have more freedom to experiment. But Mack, in his usual way, said *No*. Every once in a while, Mack had to be the stubborn Irishman to show he was the boss.

"This time Charlie wouldn't have it. He had made good money for Keystone, his face on the outside poster and the words, '*I am here today*,' were all the public needed.

"So Charlie, to everyone's surprise, simply left.

"Mack never let on, but we knew he was a man who *could* not and *would* not ever go back on his word, even if it would destroy him. That's the way he was raised—*stick to your guns. They'll eventually come around, and then you've got 'em!*

"Well, not with Charlie. We knew he was never going to return, no matter how bad things could turn out. We were sad, but the one who was really sad was Mabel. She didn't talk to any of us for the rest of the day. Nobody tried to go near her or to try and cheer her up. She wasn't Madcap Mabel that day. No jokes. Not even a flying pie…"

The Tramp had taken the road in search of another adventure. Sennett's *laissez faire* attitude regarding his players would now be tested with a new arrival.

Her name was Mae Busch, and her unwanted presence would permanently destroy the lives of Mack and Mabel.

Chapter 11
The *Ever-Popular* Mae Busch

"Whenever television comedian Jackie Gleason wanted to be sure of getting a laugh during his Saturday night television variety show, he would do his monologue as a late-night master of ceremonies presenting old movies.

"The emcee's name was Stanley R. Sogg, and he'd rattle off a long list of B players, maybe a good dozen who were playing supporting roles in Poverty Row studios. He'd say their names without even pausing for breath. And then he'd *stop*, and say, 'And the ever-popular *M-m-m-m-m-ae* Bus*ch-h-h-h-h*, who was a joke on the lot in her Sennett days.

"To those of us from those days, she wasn't a source of laughter, even though she was a comedienne, who became a bigger name when she played one of the wives in Laurel and Hardy films at the Roach Studios in the thirties. At Sennett's, she was the source of *very big* trouble!"

—Minta Durfee Arbuckle
Conversation with the author, July 1969

Had it not been an invitation from Mabel Normand, a friend of Mae's from her days at Vitagraph, Mae would have never taken the train to California.

Adela Rogers St. John explained this aspect of Mabel's character.

> "Mabel was like Fanny Brice, the *Follies* girl, who had a huge radio career playing Baby Snooks to a new generation. Fanny paid *Follies* girl Ann Pennington's train fare to California, hoping she could start her career all over again. They were in the Follies together, but Penny gambled away a lot of her money, and got involved with the wrong kind of men, something which a lot of those girls did.
>
> "When Penny moved in with Fanny, Fanny had a new wardrobe for her that she created by simply removing the labels from new dresses, and saying they were slightly, so Penny wouldn't feel that uncomfortable.
>
> "She even tried to get Penny some roles in films. Mabel felt just as sorry for her friend, Mae Busch, who was also having hard times. There are some people in show business who are like that. They'll help you on the way up, the way Al Jolson would sometimes do, and they'll help you when you are down and out. He'd sit by your bed.
>
> "Mabel tried to help Mae Busch, not really knowing what Mae Busch was *really* like. And when Mabel found out, it was too late, she was shattered. Mabel could be generous to a fault."

The Edendale gates at Sennett's were like revolving doors. Sennett himself would often say he was a "hard Irishman" who would never go back on his opinion, but he would *rehire some* of those he let go...until the subject of money reared its ugly head. He maintained that the principle of interchangeable parts (his Kops) would carry him through.

While he was disappointed that his recent loss (Hank Mann) seemed a *personal* one, he knew that Mann's going to work at Henry Lehrman's rival studio would not last very long, there was always somebody new.

In this case, it was Mae Busch, who was recommended by Mabel Normand. Mabel, Mack remembered, had brought him Chaplin, and if she turned out as well as Charlie did...

Adela Rogers St. Johns continues:

> "Mack, at Mabel's suggestion, went to the beach when Mae Busch and Mabel were there. One look at Mae on the beach in a daring swimsuit was all he needed to see..."

In response to Mabel's question, Mack gave a most definite *Yes*!

Hoping to help Mae adjust to the California lifestyle and meet some of the Sennett film community, Roscoe and Minta Arbuckle would include Mae for dinners at Minta's parents' home on N. Coronado Street in the Echo Park district. The Arbuckle home was cozy, and it was close to the studio.

Sometimes, at the end of the shooting day, Mack's touring car and chauffeur would take the Arbuckles, Mabel, Mae Busch, and the newest contract player, Anne Luther, to the public beach at Santa Monica. Although the beach at Malibu was more private and more desirable, the distance and the dirt roads made the trek something not ultimately fun—especially at the end of the day, when the shooting would continue tomorrow. While the public might enjoy watching their screen favorites at work, at play, the Malibu community didn't share their enthusiasm. Actors meant crowds who might attract crowds, and the beach could be littered.

The group emerging from the touring would change into beachfront attire at the Oceanside bungalow of Minta's parents, swim for an hour, and the chauffeur would drop everyone off at their homes.

On one of the trips back from the beach, when Mack *wasn't* present, Mabel made a surprise announcement to the Arbuckles and Anne Luther.

Minta recalled:

> "We knew the Mack and Mabel relationship was always subject to change. Sometimes on a daily basis. We stopped looking every morning to see if she were sporting that *doorknob* of an engagement ring she never really liked.
>
> "And I remember when she and Roscoe were filming *The Little Teacher*, the two of them, Mack *and* Mabel, had an on-the-set fight that could have turned into a real tavern brawl... They had been going around together for seven years, and Mabel must have *really* put her foot down. We could hear her yelling, 'It's *now* or *never*! And I'm tired of your mother, and I'm sick of seeing how you kowtow to her whenever she's around. How long is it going to be before you realize I'm not going to sit around and wait any longer?'
>
> "So Mack finally asked the question and Mabel, not wanting to look foolish any longer, asked Mack to set *the date*."

Mack set the date—July 4. It was a date that was easy to remember, even though Mack was a Canadian.

Minta recalled:

> "Mack and Mabel were still living separately. Two different addresses. None of us would have paid any attention if they had moved

in together. They certainly had been going around long enough. We always thought he was afraid of his mother, but she wasn't afraid to accept the checks he'd send to her. That was just fine.

"As a couple, the movie magazines left them alone. She would sometimes have an article written about her, but if they mentioned Mack, it was all very *professional*. Good friends and all that.

"The trips to the beach with Anne Luther and Mae Busch still continued. Sometimes the group didn't include Mae Busch. She said she had things to do, and we just had extra room that day. At the studio, Charlie Murray, who had doubts about Mack, was pleased to see his *little girl* was finally tying the knot with someone she waited so long to *finally* come around. Privately, he had told Chester Conklin that he had his doubts and that Mack's *mother* would be running the ranch. Charlie, being a gentleman, kept those thoughts to himself, and everything at Keystone was business as usual.

"And then, close to the July 4 wedding, there was a telephone call which signaled there was trouble in paradise. It was the beginning of the end."

Chapter 12
A Phone Call

Mabel lived alone in an apartment on Seventh and Figueroa. Close to her bed was a night table that held a telephone and books on her favorite topics of discussion she would have with her friend, director William Desmond Taylor—the history of the British Parliament and the French language and grammar. To her close friends, these were odd choices, but that was Madcap Mabel—totally lovable, and constantly unpredictable. To be her friend sometimes meant just going along with the mood of the day.

An evening with Mack sometimes meant dancing at the Vernon Country Club, or having dinner with the Arbuckles at Levy's Café, or just listening to music at Arbuckle's parents' home with Minta's parents on a Sunday evening.

Reading was Mabel's favorite way of escape. She could hide in a book when the pressures of her celebrity sometimes became unbearable. Reading about her *madcap* life, as depicted in the film magazines, had little resemblance to her reality. Often she would say to Minta, "I'd like to be that person," and Minta would reply, "Dear, so would we all…"

The telephone ringing late at night had awakened Mabel from a deep sleep. The voice on the end was hysterical and almost unrecognizable as it shrieked into her ear. Seconds later, fully awake, Mabel identified the caller as Anne Luther, with whom she had spent part of the afternoon at the beach. Anne was not shooting tomorrow, so she could go to bed late.

The message Anne had yelled into Mabel's ear was short—*Get over to Mack's hotel immediately.*

And then Anne hung up. Mabel sat up and rubbed her eyes until she was awake. Was Mack suddenly taken ill?

Fearing the worst and hoping to avoid any publicity, she called Anne back. What was wrong? Would Anne drive her to Mack's hotel and leave her? Whatever the problem was, it would not take too long to solve. Although Mabel could easily summon a limousine, their drivers were easily bribed, and were often notorious sources of gossip, as were taxi drivers. Maybe Mack had had another telephone argument with his mother. Maybe she was threatening him with another visit. Maybe she was going to pressure him not to marry Mabel, that *actress*!

Anne drove Mabel to Mack's hotel, and Mabel hurried up to Mack's suite. She knocked on the door, and Mack, thinking it was the bellhop with liquor and sandwiches, answered. He was dressed only in the bottoms of his underwear.

Both of their faces registered shock and surprise. *Who had sent for Mabel?* Mabel looked past Mack's shoulder to the living room. Somebody in a black negligee was trying to hide behind the sofa, but Mabel recognized who it was.

It was Mae Busch!

Before Mack could say anything, the vase that was over the fireplace suddenly went flying across the room aimed at Mabel with deadly accuracy at her forehead.

It was a direct hit. Mabel fell, spattering her blood all over the living room rug. Minutes later she rose, pushing away Mack, who had been holding a towel to the center of her forehead, and staggered past him to the elevator.

With her face covered, Mabel was unrecognizable, even to the few who were sitting in the lobby.

By this time, Anne Luther's car had gone. A taxi driver, someone she had hoped to avoid, was parked in Anne's place. Keeping the towel over her face, she entered the taxi and told the driver *not* to take her to the hospital, but to the Arbuckle house on Coronado Street.

The driver, seeing the large bill, knew not to ask any questions. There was only the matter of the reddened towel, but the passenger seemed to have everything under control. She had curled herself in the corner of the taxi, and she had kept her face covered. Only one eye was visible…

It was a hot evening, Minta remembered, and she and Roscoe were sleeping on the porch on chaise lounges when the taxi turned onto the driveway, and they were awakened by the sounds of screaming.

Minta told this author:

> "In the middle of our sleep, we heard what we thought was a suffering animal. We saw the door of the taxi opening, and the driver carrying Mabel cradled in his arms like a newborn baby up to our porch. There was blood all over Mabel's face and hair, streaming down her neck and all over the front of her body.
>
> "Naturally, we paid the driver something extra, hoping he would keep silent...
>
> "After the taxi left, Mabel told us, as best as she could, what had happened at Mack's, that she caught Mae Busch there, and that Mae had thrown a large vase directly at her head. Roscoe wanted to take Mabel to the hospital, but I telephoned Nell Ince [the wife of studio head Thomas Ince, whose Inceville studio produced mostly Westerns in the area of the Santa Inez Canyon near Malibu], who told me she knew a *discreet* doctor who had helped women with *other* problems, and could be trusted.
>
> "Mabel was still hemorrhaging when Nell and the doctor arrived. Her pillow, on which her head was resting, was soaked with blood. The doctor told us if we wanted Mabel to be alive in the morning, we'd have to check her into a hospital immediately.

"He checked Mabel into a hospital, but we had to drive Mabel there ourselves, following his car. The doctor took care of the details.

"Instead of waking up, Mabel lapsed into a coma, and Nell and I alternated shifts in addition to the regular nurses. There were no reporters, and surprisingly, no sign of Mack! Not even a telephone call the *next* day!

"After two weeks of no improvement, the doctor told us an operation was necessary, if we wanted to save Mabel's life. The blood would have to be drained out of the top of her head, and he couldn't guarantee her behavior afterwards.

"On the morning of the operation, I first reported for work. Everyone was standing around, and there was silence. Finally, Mack came in and yelled, 'What the hell's going on around here. Is this a work day or not?'

"Charlie Murray, who was a few years older than most of us and loved Mabel like a daughter, stepped up to where Mack was standing. He grabbed him by the shirt collar, and looked him right in the eye. 'If that little girl dies, you no-count son-of-a-bitch, you had better keep out of our way!'"

Chapter 13
Marking Time...

"Hollywood has always been a town of secrets.
Some you can believe, and some you can't.
Even when they reach print."

—Adela Rogers St. John
Conversation with author, August 1974

Readers of the September 30, 1915 edition of the *Santa Monica Outlook* were shocked to read of Mabel Normand's *accident* on the Edendale lot. The reason for not reporting to work was easily explained: she had been hurt during the shooting of a wedding scene.

Nothing was needed of additional explanation. *Madcap Mabel*, the studio hellion, had taken a dive off the Santa Monica Pier!

She stayed in seclusion at her apartment for three months. When she returned for work, to honor her contract, her *professional* contract, she was no longer the same friendly good-humored Mabel she had been until the encountered with Mae Busch in Mack's room before the wedding.

Both Minta's and Mack's mother tried to persuade Mabel to let the planned wedding continue.

Catherine Sinnott had a simple explanation for what had happened—Mack had been a bachelor for so long, he was just exercising a man's prerogative, as many bachelors sometimes do just before they get married. It was a *last fling*, a last opportunity to have a good time before he had to settle down.

Nobody listening to her paid much attention. They had a workday to get through—features and two-reelers had to be completed by the deadline for distribution had passed.

Minta told this writer:

> "When Mabel came back, her face was gaunt, and she was without any expression. The laugh factory had suddenly become any old factory where the morale was low, and nobody wanted to really be there but for the money.
>
> "There was a *Did you see her?* and *How do you think she looked?* unvoiced question that we didn't want to have answered, because we knew what it would be. It was like responses at a wake—you don't cry until you see somebody else crying, and your own embarrassment and sudden self-consciousness are gone.
>
> "Mabel's on-the-set courtesies and manners were quieter and softer. *She* wanted to talk, and *we* wanted to talk, but we didn't want to speak the obvious to each other. Our eyes said it all, and we sensed each other's pain. Talk wasn't necessary.
>
> "Mack wasn't around when the actual shooting began, and when he finally reported on the set, he *too* was subdued. To him, we merely nodded and kept silent. Words weren't necessary.
>
> "Mabel whispered that Mack kept sending her flowers everyday, and she kept refusing them and sending them back. If she kept those flowers, her bed at the hospital would

have resembled a casket at a funeral parlor, and she wasn't going to give him or his mother the satisfaction of dying.

"'Mack never knew what love is. A wedding ring or not, he's a big Mama's boy. He's put me through enough. She wants him? She can have him!'"

In yet another effort to win Mabel back to his life and return to the relationship they once had, Sennett filmed *Mickey*, a six-reeler that tried to show a different side of Mabel, *not* her Madcap Mabel character, but a Mabel with warmth.

While the film was a success and it gave her considerable money (for always thrifty Mack) she wasn't aware of the recent ramifications of Keystone's merge with Triangle Productions.

Mack was no longer in charge. He was an *employee*, and lucky to be one.

What Mack wasn't aware of was Mabel's plans to leave him, and go with Samuel Goldwyn, a producer who was always very fond of her. Working at Goldwyn's was Mabel's opportunity to get away from Mack's double-dealings, false promises, personal frustrations, and…Mama.

Mabel's departure was, on the surface, strictly professional, but Mack knew he would never win her back. She had been bruised too often.

Sign with Sennett, get rich someplace else.

His greatest loss, the loss from which he would never recover was Mabel. He would remain a bachelor for the rest of his life.

Mabel was his great love, he would tell anyone who would listen…until people grew too tired of hearing his laments of an over-aged lovesick swain.

Still, there was always the money. Any money. So long as he was able to earn money, Mama was happy. When Mama was happy, he was happy.

No matter who that studio player was, that person could always be replaced, and the replacement would always work cheaper…for a while.

Mack knew ultimately that one can only survive as long as they turned out a product that made money. It wasn't show *art*, it was show *money*.

So long as he could save money, he had money.

Mack knew Mama was right.

Always...

Bibliography

Alexandta, Virginia. *One-Hundred Years of Hollywood.* Loretta Britten, Paul Mathess, editors. New York: Time-Life Books, 1999
Allen, Frederick Lewis. *Only Yesterday.* New York: Bantam, 1946.
Basten, Fred E. *Beverly Hills.* Los Angeles: Douglas-West Publishers, 1975.
_____.*Santa Monica Bay.* Los Angeles, California: Douglas-West Publishers, 1975
Blum, Daniel, ed., *A Pictorial History of the American Theatre.* New York: Crown, 1969.
Cassara, Bill. *Edgar Kennedy, Master of the Slow Burn.* Albany, Georgia: BearManor Media, 2005.
Chaplin, Charles. *My Autobiography.* New York: Simon and Schuster, 1964.
Fussell, Better Harper. *Mabel.* New York: Ticknor and Fields, 1982.
Green, Abel and Joe Laurie, Jr. *Show Biz: From Vaude to Video.* New York: Henry Hold, 1957.
Griffith, Richard and Arthur Mayer. *The Movies.* New York: Simon and Schuster, 1957.
Huff, Theodore. *Charlie Chaplin.* New York: Arno Press, 1972.
Jacobs, Lewis. *The Rise of the American Film: A Critical History.* New York: Harcourt, Brace, 1939.
Kerr, Walter. *The Silent Clowns.* New York: Alfred A. Knopf, 1975.
Lahue, Katlon C. *Mack Sennett's Keystone: The Man, the Myth, and the Comedies.* South Brunswick and New York: A.S. Barnes and Company, 1972.
_____. *World of Laughter: the Motion Picture Comedy Short*, 1910-1930. University of Oklahoma Press, 1966.

_____.and Terry Brewer. *Kops and Custards: The Legend of Keystone Films.* University of Oklahoma Press, 1968.

and Samuel Gill. *Clown Princes and Court Jesters.* South Brunswick and New York: A.S. Barnes, 1970.

Louvish, Simon. *Keystone: The Life and Clowns of Mack Sennett.* New York: Faber & Faber, 2003.

Maltin, Leonard. *The Great Movie Comedians.* New York: Crown, 1978.

Oderman, Stuart. *Lillian Gish: A Life on Stage and Screen.* Jefferson, North Carolina. McFarland, 1994.

_____.*Roscoe "Fatty" Arbuckle: A Biography of the Silent Film Comedian, 1887-1933.* McFarland, 1994.

_____.*Talking to the Piano Player: Silent Film Stars, Writers and Directors Remember.* Albany, Georgia: BearManor Media, 2005.

Ramsaye, Terry. *A Million and One Nights: A History of the Motion Picture Through 1925.* New York: Simon and Schuster, 1964.

Slide, Anthony. *Early American Cinema.* New York: A.S. Barnes and Co., 1970.

Seldes, Gilbert. *The Seven Lively Arts.* New York: Sagamore Press, 1957.

Sennett, Mack, as told to Cameron Shipp. *King of Comedy.* New York: Doubleday and Co., 1954.

Swanson, Gloria. *Swanson on Swanson: An Autobiography.* London: Michael Joseph, 1981.

Talbot, Daniel, editor. *Film: An Anthology: 1959.* Berkeley, California: University of California Press, 1959.

Taylor, Deems, Marceline Peterson, and Bryant Hall. *A Pictorial History of Movies.* New York: Simon and Schuster, 1950.

Here's a small sampling of a few more books published by BearManor Media.

Simply go online for details about these and other terrific titles.

www.BearManorMedia.com

Silent Stars Speak!
New CD

Thrill to actual voices of the world's greatest stars on *Silent Movie Stars Speak*, a compilation of rare recordings of 21 of the greatest stars of the silent film era. You'll hear these fascinating, lost interviews:

- BLANCHE SWEET RECALLING WORKING ON BIOGRAPH FILMS WITH D. W. GRIFFITH
- LILLIAN GISH REMINISCING ABOUT HER FIRST FILM WITH HER SISTER, DOROTHY GISH.
- HAROLD LLOYD REMEMBERING HOW HE PROGRESSED FROM HIS EARLY BEGINNINGS.
- STAN LAUREL THINKING BACK TO BOYHOOD TOURS AND WORKING WITH OLIVER HARDY.
- BUSTER KEATON REVEALING HOW HE BECAME "THE GREAT STONEFACE" IN FILMS.
- JOHN AND LIONEL BARRYMORE TELLING HOW THEY ROSE FROM OBSCURITY TO FAME.
- BRONCO BILLY'S THRILLING RECOUNT OF MAKING *THE GREAT TRAIN ROBBERY*.

You will also witness first-hand performances given on wax cylinder records, 78 rpm records, film, or on live radio broadcasts Ramon Novarro, Mary Pickford, Jackie Coogan, Charlie Chaplin, Laurette Taylor, Sarah Bernhardt, Douglas Fairbanks, Gloria Swanson, John Gilbert, and Greta Garbo. In the finale, William S. Hart is heard in the heartrending speech he gave in a Prologue for the 1930s re-release of his film, *Tumbleweeds*.

Each recording has been digitally re-mastered to improve clarity. They vary in quality, and on some tracks there is slight surface noise that cannot be removed without damaging the recording, but on each, the voices of the great stars come through loudly and clearly.

New CD in factory shrink-wrap. $12.95 + postage
Postage $4.95 on Priority Mail inside the USA only.
$12.00 Global Priority mail outside the USA.
$10.00 Air Mail for Italy only.

BearManor Media · PO Box 71426 · Albany, GA 31708
e-mail: books@benohmart.com
Telephone: 229.436.4265 · Toll Free: 1.800.566.1251 · Fax: 814.690.1559
Or online at: www.bearmanormedia.com

Silent Movie Stars Speak

The Lost Recordings of Hollywood's Greatest Stars

ETHEL BARRYMORE	DOUGLAS FAIRBANKS	STAN LAUREL
LIONEL BARRYMORE	GRETA GARBO	HAROLD LLOYD
JOHN BARRYMORE	JOHN GILBERT	RAMON NOVARRO
SARAH BERNHARDT	LILLIAN GISH	MARY PICKFORD
BRONCO BILLY	D.W. GRIFFITH	GLORIA SWANSON
CHARLIE CHAPLIN	WILLIAM S. HART	BLANCHE SWEET
JACKIE COOGAN	BUSTER KEATON	LAURETTE TAYLOR

Track 1	2:00	RAMON NOVARRO
Track 2	0.59	BLANCHE SWEET
Track 3	6:47	HAROLD LLOYD
Track 4	5:52	MARY PICKFORD
Track 5	4:56	STAN LAUREL
Track 6	2:55	JACKIE COOGAN (WITH HIS FATHER)
Track 7	5:19	BUSTER KEATON
Track 8	2:47	CHARLIE CHAPLIN
Track 9	0:54	ETHEL BARRYMORE
Track 10	1:36	LIONEL BARRYMORE
Track 11	2:00	JOHN BARRYMORE
Track 12	3:29	LAURETTE TAYLOR
Track 13	0:58	BRONCO BILLY ANDERSON
Track 14	4:03	SARAH BERNHARDT
Track 15	2:23	D. W. GRIFFITH (WITH WALTER HOUSTON)
Track 16	2:23	LILLIAN GISH
Track 17	2:08	DOUGLAS FAIRBANKS
Track 18	3:30	GLORIA SWANSON
Track 19	4:02	JOHN GILBERT
Track 20	3:59	GRETA GARBO
Track 21	7:28	WILLIAM S. HART

www.ingramcontent.com/pod-product-compliance
Lightning Source LLC
Chambersburg PA
CBHW020759160426
43192CB00006B/380